"As an emotionally sensitive p
outstanding job of addressing
and compassion. *The Emotionally Sensitive Person* provides a practical guide for successful coping that also serves to inspire. Highly recommended."

—**Amanda L. Smith**, dialectical behavior therapy (DBT) therapist and treatment consultant

"*The Emotionally Sensitive Person* is exceptional. This unique manual, compassionately written by Karyn D. Hall, will appeal to and serve the needs of those who live with highly sensitive emotions. She highlights proven methods to consciously and skillfully manage unhelpful thoughts and behaviors by following and practicing personalized exercises. Read, practice, experience, and enjoy *The Emotionally Sensitive Person* as you learn new ways to enhance your life."

—**Diane and Jim Hall**, educators for National Alliance on Mental Illness Family-to-Family and NEA.BPD's Family Connections programs

"Emotionally sensitive people will want to keep this compassionate, instructional guidebook on their nightstands. Hall's clinical wisdom shines through as she offers numerous helpful tools, informed by dialectical behavior therapy, to be used immediately to better cope with one's emotional states. I will recommend this self-help book to my own clients to complement and enhance the psychotherapy."

—**Alec L. Miller, PsyD**, professor of clinical psychiatry and behavioral sciences, Montefiore Medical Center, Albert Einstein College of Medicine, and cofounder, Cognitive and Behavioral Consultants, LLP

"This book takes readers by the hand and gently introduces them to the struggle, suffering, and hidden potential of the emotionally sensitive person. Drawing from her wealth of clinical experience, Hall presents essential strategies to support the development of emotional sensitivity into a strength. The chapters are well organized and concisely written. Therapeutic exercises are practical with clear and concise instructions. Anyone who has been accused of being 'too sensitive' can benefit from this book!"

—**Elizabeth W. Newlin, MD**, assistant professor in the Menninger department of psychiatry and behavioral sciences at Baylor College of Medicine and director of the adolescent treatment program at the Menninger Clinic

"For anyone who's ever thought of themselves as emotionally sensitive—or someone who's lived with someone who is—this book is an invaluable gem. Using proven therapeutic techniques, Hall delivers on helping people keep their emotional sensitivity, but honing it so that it is more beneficial than hurtful. I can't imagine a better resource for those who are grappling with this issue in their lives."

—**John M. Grohol, PsyD**, founder and CEO of psychcentral.com, the Internet's leading mental health site

"Karyn D. Hall brings a wealth of wisdom and experience to the pages of her new book, *The Emotionally Sensitive Person*. With practical advice and useful exercises, she teaches us how to dismantle an emotional roller coaster style and to replace it with just the right amount of sensitivity and feeling. Highly recommended!"

—**John M. Oldham, MD**, chief of staff at the Menninger Clinic and professor of psychiatry at Baylor College of Medicine

The Emotionally Sensitive Person

FINDING *Peace* WHEN YOUR EMOTIONS OVERWHELM YOU

KARYN D. HALL, PhD

New Harbinger Publications, Inc.

Publisher's Note

This publication is designed to provide accurate and authoritative information in regard to the subject matter covered. It is sold with the understanding that the publisher is not engaged in rendering psychological, financial, legal, or other professional services. If expert assistance or counseling is needed, the services of a competent professional should be sought.

Distributed in Canada by Raincoast Books

New Harbinger Publications, Inc.
5674 Shattuck Avenue
Oakland, CA 94609
www.newharbinger.com

Cover design by Amy Shoup; Acquired by Melissa Kirk; Edited by Will DeRooy

Library of Congress Cataloging-in-Publication Data on file

FSC
www.fsc.org
MIX
Paper from responsible sources
FSC® C011935

RAINFOREST ALLIANCE CERTIFIED

Printed in the United States of America

16 15 14

10 9 8 7 6 5 4 3 2 1 First printing

For Chris

Contents

Acknowledgments

I'm grateful to so many who supported and contributed to this project. Emotionally sensitive people all over the world shared generously and bravely about living with emotional sensitivity. Please know that all examples represent a combination of different people's experiences. All names have been altered, and any resemblance to any single individual is conincidental.

My thinking is heavily influenced by the work of Marsha Linehan, PhD, who created dialectical behavior therapy. Thank you also to Shari Manning, PhD, and Helen Best at Treatment Implementation Collaborative, who always encourage growth with inspiring integrity.

My gratitude to Suzanne Robinson, Kelly Guynes, Pamela Jones, Joseph Pentony, Rebecca Ciatto, Lindsay Raymer, Beverly Bontrager, Meggan Watson, and Angela Tallo, who are all a constant source of wisdom. Kraig Dunn is amazingly skillful and makes even the most outrageous ideas a reality. I'm sure he will some day find a way to have horses on the roof of our office building. Carla Sharp, PhD, and Allison Kalpakci, BS, designed a research study in addition to their already full schedules.

This book wouldn't exist without the gifted professionals at New Harbinger Publications. Thank you to Melissa Kirk and Jess Beebe in particular. Jueli Garfinkle and Will DeRooy in some magical way turned my ramblings into meaningful text. This book makes sense because of them.

I'm grateful to my friends and family members who accepted the long hours I spent writing and rewriting, especially Michelle Meisenhalder and Ray and Barbara Meisenhalder. I am always and forever grateful to Chris, who unconditionally helps me pursue my dreams.

Introduction

Emotionally sensitive people are those who experience intense emotions more frequently and for longer periods of time than most people do. Given that you've picked up this book, chances are that you see yourself or someone you know as emotionally sensitive.

Perhaps you recognize the challenges faced by Alisha, Harold, or Nicole:

When Alisha found out that Roger had cheated on her repeatedly throughout their marriage, she filed for divorce. Yet she couldn't bring herself to ask him to move out of the house—in addition to fearing that he would be upset with her, she was worried about how she would feel without him around. So now, a couple of years later, they still live together, and she supports him. After all, she explains to her friends, he has no place to go and has difficulty managing his money. She hates that her fear of feeling bad keeps her from making the decision she knows makes the most sense (i.e., to ask him to leave). She realizes it shows a lack of self-respect.

Harold worries about unintentionally offending others and struggles with saying no. He stays on the phone for hours with upset friends and acquaintances to the point he isn't getting daily tasks completed. He doesn't watch the news because it makes him sad.

Nicole sees herself as weak, as "not good enough." She's often in tears, angry, or sad when no one else is. Others tell her she "wears her heart on her sleeve" and "lets everything get to her." These comments and many more make her feel different and misunderstood.

Do any of these stories sound familiar? Even if they're not right on target, read on. There are different ways of being emotionally sensitive, and you may not have the same pattern of emotional sensitivity as Alisha, Harold, or Nicole.

Are You Emotionally Sensitive?

Through interviews, surveys, and years of clinical work, I've found that emotionally sensitive people vary in the way they interact with others. For example, you may hide most of your anger and irritation. Or maybe you are openly irritated and angry much of the time, like a porcupine with its quills up. You may be friends with everyone you meet, or you may isolate yourself. However, most emotionally sensitive people share certain characteristics.

The following questionnaire may help you determine whether you're emotionally sensitive. For each statement, circle the answer that best indicates to what extent this has been your experience.

Emotional Sensitivity Self-Assessment

1. I'm often told by people who know me well that I'm too sensitive.

   1 Strongly Disagree 2 Disagree 3 Agree 4 Strongly Agree

2. I often worry about hurting other people's feelings.

   1 Strongly Disagree 2 Disagree 3 Agree 4 Strongly Agree

3. If I'm asked where I'd like to go to lunch, either I say "I don't know" or I choose where I think the other person wants to go, because I want to make others happy.

   1 Strongly Disagree 2 Disagree 3 Agree 4 Strongly Agree

4. Making decisions is difficult for me.

   1 Strongly Disagree 2 Disagree 3 Agree 4 Strongly Agree

5. If something unfair happens, I have a hard time letting it go.

   1 Strongly Disagree 2 Disagree 3 Agree 4 Strongly Agree

6. Nature is particularly grounding and calming for me.

   1 Strongly Disagree 2 Disagree 3 Agree 4 Strongly Agree

7. When other people are upset, I get upset too.

   1 Strongly Disagree 2 Disagree 3 Agree 4 Strongly Agree

8. I try to avoid or hide my emotions.

   1 Strongly Disagree 2 Disagree 3 Agree 4 Strongly Agree

9. I change to fit in with the people I'm with.

   1 Strongly Disagree 2 Disagree 3 Agree 4 Strongly Agree

10. If a friend doesn't return my call or text, I assume she's angry with me.

    1 Strongly Disagree 2 Disagree 3 Agree 4 Strongly Agree

11. I have more intense reactions to bad news than most people do.

    1 Strongly Disagree 2 Disagree 3 Agree 4 Strongly Agree

12. When I'm emotional, I have difficulty thinking. My brain shuts down.

    1 Strongly Disagree 2 Disagree 3 Agree 4 Strongly Agree

13. I avoid projects and social activities because I'm afraid of being criticized.

    1 Strongly Disagree 2 Disagree 3 Agree 4 Strongly Agree

14. I often cancel plans with friends because I don't feel like being with them.

    1 Strongly Disagree 2 Disagree 3 Agree 4 Strongly Agree

15. I shop too much, drink too much, work too much, eat too much, or sleep too much.

    1 Strongly Disagree 2 Disagree 3 Agree 4 Strongly Agree

16. I often don't know what emotion I'm feeling or why I'm feeling a certain way.

    1 Strongly Disagree 2 Disagree 3 Agree 4 Strongly Agree

17. Other people are usually jerks who are out to make life hard for me.

    1 Strongly Disagree 2 Disagree 3 Agree 4 Strongly Agree

18. I really don't know what other people see in me or why they'd want to be around me.

    1 Strongly Disagree 2 Disagree 3 Agree 4 Strongly Agree

19. Change scares me.

    1 Strongly Disagree 2 Disagree 3 Agree 4 Strongly Agree

20. I hate myself and how emotional I am.

    1 Strongly Disagree 2 Disagree 3 Agree 4 Strongly Agree

Scoring: Add your points for each question. Note that item 20 has higher points for the Agree and Strongly Agree options.

70–82 Strongly emotionally sensitive

55–69 Emotionally sensitive

45–54 Mildly emotionally sensitive

20–44 Not emotionally sensitive

The Gift and Curse of Sensitive Emotions

Being emotionally sensitive can be both a gift and a burden. If your emotions repeatedly overwhelm you, you may not view your intense feelings as a gift. Yet your caring about others, your intense joy, your strong feelings of connectedness, and your passionate nature can add a sense of purpose, meaning, and contentment to your life.

Learning to manage your intense emotions is key to reducing your suffering and helping you enjoy more of the gifts of emotional sensitivity. Managing your emotions involves recognizing and accepting your emotions, using healthy strategies to cope with uncomfortable emotions, and choosing behaviors that will move your life forward instead of pushing you deeper into chaos. For example, repeatedly agreeing to babysit active children when you don't feel well, inviting relatives who criticize your every move to stay in your home, shopping to the point that you can't pay your bills, eating too much, and yelling at people you love are all ways you might act on emotions in ways that make your life more difficult.

Managing your emotions is critical for living well, but there's no course in school (that I know of) called Managing Your Emotions 101. Plus, most parents don't talk with their children about (or model how to handle) sad, hurt, or angry feelings. Explaining how to cope with strong emotions is difficult. If you ask people how they cope when they've been rejected for a job they wanted or when a beloved friend isn't speaking to them, you'll get a variety of answers. Some will say they don't worry about it or that it's no big deal. Some will say they just forget about it. Most likely you'll be told that time is a great healer. And it is. But if you're emotionally sensitive, these events aren't minor bumps in the road, and the pain you feel while waiting for the emotion to pass can seem unbearable.

What to Expect from This Book

As you read this book, you'll learn the characteristics of emotionally sensitive people. You'll understand both general and specific ways to manage your intense feelings so that you're able to make more effective choices and improve your personal and work relationships. You'll practice strategies for decreasing the intensity of your emotions, thinking before you act, and recognizing what you're feeling.

Some strategies will likely work better than others, and most will be more effective after you've practiced them for a while. *Practice* is a key word. Overcoming your typical patterns of behavior won't be easy. But the human brain is more flexible than we used to believe. By learning to cope with strong emotions, you can change your mental habits so that you no longer respond automatically in ways that make the situation worse, such as overeating or isolating yourself.

Go through this book slowly. Complete the exercises in each chapter. When you read the sections that describe skills or ideas that could be helpful, stop. Practice the ideas for a few weeks. Then, after you're regularly using what you've learned, move on to the next section. The results will be well worth the time and effort, because your daily life will become easier and more enjoyable when your emotions no longer control you.

CHAPTER 1

Understanding Emotional Sensitivity

If you're emotionally sensitive, your emotions tend to come on more quickly, be more intense, and last longer than other people's emotions. You probably struggle each day to cope with your feelings. You may not trust yourself because you can't predict how you'll react in different situations. Many times, acting on your emotions adds anguish and trouble to your life.

People in your life may not understand or accept the intensity of your emotions. Perhaps they tell you that you're overreacting, too sensitive, or too dramatic. You may see yourself as different from other people, most likely in a negative way. You may dislike yourself or even hate yourself and the pain you experience.

At the same time, you may cherish being emotionally sensitive. Perhaps your connections with and compassion for other people are a source of great joy. You'd like to drop the painful emotions, but keep your capacity for connection, compassion, and joy.

Part of learning how to cope with your emotions is to understand the characteristics of emotionally sensitive people. Feeling understood, learning that others share your experiences, and accepting your emotional sensitivity will establish the groundwork.

Traits of Emotionally Sensitive People

Most of the traits of emotionally sensitive people have both an upside and a downside. Some emotionally sensitive people experience more of the positive effects of being emotionally sensitive, while others struggle with the difficult consequences and rarely notice the benefits.

A Deeply Sensitive Perspective on the Natural World

For emotionally sensitive people, almost every interaction and event is marked with emotion. Your strong emotions mean you feel wonderfully alive. Simple events, such as watching the wind toss a balloon, can be a moving experience. At the same time, feeling such strong emotions can be exhausting. Finding peace can be a challenge.

If you're emotionally sensitive, nature may ground and calm you. A connection to nature can offer you a sense of belonging and not being alone. Smelling a flower, hearing the ocean waves, viewing fall foliage, or snuggling a pet can replenish you when you feel drained. In fact, emotionally sensitive people may gain a great deal of comfort from their pets and, in turn, give them exceptional care. On the other hand, a love of nature also means it may pain you when nature isn't respected by others. When others laughed at the chimpanzees playing at the zoo, you may have felt sad they were in a cage. Seeing animals hurt may enrage you or send you into deep sadness. As a child, you may even have been concerned about plants, fearful if you walked on grass you'd hurt it.

Sensitivity to Others' Emotions

Emotionally sensitive people are highly alert to the emotions of others. If you're emotionally sensitive, any time others are upset, you may feel just as upset as they do (or more so). When someone needs comforting, you probably know exactly what to say. When you see someone crying, you may be concerned about that person for hours. As a child, you may have worried about the teacher's feelings when your classmates misbehaved and worried about your parents' finances when you needed expensive supplies for school. You're especially talented at making people feel welcome and at giving meaningful presents. You can be a loyal ally. When a friend is beaten down by life and others have stopped calling him, you remain by his side. When help is needed, you're there.

The fact that you're acutely attuned to others' emotions, however, can mean that people have far too much influence on your feelings. You may overanalyze people's words and behaviors and often be suspicious and worried about what others think of you. You may be so concerned about hurting others that you don't stand up for yourself at times. You may attempt to solve problems for those who are in pain, even if it means giving in to their wants when you shouldn't. You may have strong physical reactions, such as an upset stomach or even vomiting, when you must carry out personal or business tasks that might upset the people involved.

Excessive Tolerance and Intolerance

The caring that emotionally sensitive people feel, along with the fact that they're easily hurt, results in significant ups and downs in their relationships. If you're emotionally sensitive, you may have a strong need to have people in your life but also a reactive nature. It may be difficult to decide what's too much to tolerate from others and what to overlook. You may make excuses for those who behave badly. Perhaps you don't see the way someone treats you as negative, though others do, or you don't believe you deserve better. Maybe you think being with someone who's unkind is better than being alone.

You may also react easily and strongly to small annoyances and repeatedly think about ending relationships over issues that wouldn't bother others. You can be very distrustful, even of those who are closest to you. You may be so suspicious that you're angry most of the time, seeing people as judgmental and unfair.

Sometimes emotionally sensitive people become worn out and avoid everyone. Listening to heartbreak and troubles can be stressful and emotionally fatiguing, as can being stressed about how others are treating you. You may get to the point you simply can't listen to another word or you just want to be alone.

A Love/Hate Relationship with One's Own Emotions

If you're emotionally sensitive, you're probably grateful to have intense joy, happiness, love, and excitement, as well as the ability to connect with and care about others, and unpleasant emotions can be agonizing. In any given situation, you can't predict how upset you'll get or for how long. You don't know when you'll be emotionally overwhelmed, and your predictions about how well you can cope in various situations are often incorrect. Sometimes you may wish you didn't have feelings at all.

A major fear for many emotionally sensitive people is that their emotional reactions will cost them important relationships. Many have lost friends, family relationships, and romantic partners because of their sensitivity. You've probably vowed over and over again to not lose control and not react so quickly or so often.

Managing anger is particularly difficult. Any time you're angry, you probably want to attack. Because intense emotions can lead to misinterpretations, your anger may often be due to a misunderstanding—then you may attack when there's no reason to do so. Any time you attack with anger, it strains your relationships. Fear of conflict or poor conflict-resolution skills may pose additional barriers to resolving misunderstandings. You may decide you never want to talk with someone again, only to regret your decision a few hours later. These ups and downs with those you love can be particularly discouraging.

You may prefer to stay lonely rather than risk the pain of losing friendships and other relationships due to your emotional reactions.

Emotionally sensitive people often feel shame about being sensitive, so they try to hide their feelings. You may believe that if you show your emotions, others will see you as weak or less intelligent, particularly if you cry easily. These self-judgments can lead to rejecting your emotions, which adds to the difficulty in coping with them.

Sensitivity to Rejection

Sensitivity to rejection interferes, in many different ways, with an emotionally sensitive person's ability to live his life fully. Every interaction holds the possibility of real or perceived rejection. If you're emotionally sensitive, you may dread socializing because of the possible pain involved. Even mildly critical statements made by acquaintances may lead you to think you'll never fit in. If a friend doesn't include you in a luncheon invitation, you may believe you're being left out, even though you know she has many different friends. You might interpret someone's tone of voice as meaning he or she doesn't like you. In your head, you may go over and over conversations, fearing that you said something wrong and your friends will shun you. It may be particularly hurtful when a romantic partner doesn't call, even when you aren't sure you want to be in the relationship. Rejection sensitivity can also affect your life in other ways, such as not taking risks in school or your career because you see not succeeding as rejection.

Frequent Emotional Fatigue

Coping with persistent intense emotions can be exhausting. People who are emotionally sensitive can only spend so much time "in the world" before they need to escape the emotional overload. If you're emotionally sensitive, you may sometimes crave solitude or need to be with "safe" people to feel peaceful. Or you may find it restful to lose yourself in a busy place where no one knows you. The problem is that you may feel shame about withdrawing and then judge yourself.

Difficulty Making Decisions

If you're emotionally sensitive, you may struggle to make decisions or take action, because your intense emotions can be paralyzing and confusing. You may be plagued by self-doubt. Sometimes you may take feelings as facts: if you feel something, then it must be true. At times, you may react too swiftly without thinking through the consequences. When problems are difficult to resolve, you can be easily discouraged and give up. You may often think that life is just too hard and wish you were able to simply make decisions and move on, as everyone else seems to do.

Intuitive Thinking

Intuition is defined as the ability to understand something instinctively, without the need for conscious reasoning. Intuitive thinking is the mind working in ways we aren't aware of and often don't understand. Intuitive people often know certain things to be true, though they cannot explain how they reached that understanding—they simply have a sense of certainty. Emotionally sensitive people are typically intuitive.

You've probably experienced "knowing" that you're in danger, that someone's lying, that someone you've just met will be the love of your life, or that you should turn left at the next stoplight. You "know" a situation will work out fine or that someone shouldn't accept a proposal, all without being able to explain the logic of your decision or the reasons you "know."

Your intuitive thinking can be a valuable resource, but your strong emotions can interfere with using it. For example, anxious people can be particularly attuned to their spouse's negative feelings and thoughts and less aware of the positive ones. Being attuned to the negative, of course, will distort your picture of the relationship. Learning to use your intuition productively can thus be a challenge.

Creativity

There are many ways of being creative. If you're emotionally sensitive, you may be artistic, musically gifted, an excellent writer, or talented at interior design. You may create appealing flower arrangements or attractive outfits. Perhaps you have a vivid imagination or throw fabulous parties.

If you're emotionally sensitive, you may be particularly good at seeing the "big picture." You may exhibit an ability to put things together in unusual ways or to see how making certain changes could result in something new—meaning you often arrive at novel solutions to problems. These skills can serve you well in the business world, where innovative solutions are valued. For example, you might readily see how a faster way of cleaning the floor could be successfully advertised as a way for parents to increase the time they have to improve their children's school performance or for a person to impress a critical mother-in-law.

A Strong Sense of Justice

Emotionally sensitive people are passionate about injustice, whether it affects them directly or not. They're upset when they see actions that they think aren't fair, and they're ready to stand up for the person they think was wronged. Sometimes this can result in an emotionally sensitive person fighting battles for others that those people need to fight for themselves. For example, if you're emotionally sensitive, maybe you've called your son's school to argue that he shouldn't be counted tardy because his brother was the one who made him late. Although others may view your efforts to make life fair and to protect people as controlling or overinvolved, you don't see how anyone could let injustices happen without taking a stand.

A Fluid Identity

Your personal identity is your understanding of who you are as a person. It includes your likes and dislikes, your values, and your personality characteristics. Intense emotions can interfere with understanding who you are and developing a core set of values that serves as a guide for living your life. Emotionally sensitive people may feel adrift in life, pushed here and there by who and what comes their way.

One emotionally sensitive person described it to me this way: "I'm not sure who I am; sometimes I'm who I need to be for that situation." Others say "I'm still trying to discover myself" and "I feel I tend to flip-flop. I try to be what others want, until the real me becomes invisible."

Because emotions give you important information about your identity, it's important to both experience and manage them. If you don't let yourself feel emotion, then you won't receive the necessary feedback to accurately judge what you like and dislike. If on the other hand your emotions are overwhelming, it may be hard to hear exactly what they're telling you.

Without a solid identity, your sense of who you are can change depending on who you're with, what book you read, or where you are. Like a chameleon, you change to fit in with those around you. On one day, you may be sure that you're an environmentalist who wants to live off the land, but then a week later you may be passionate about devoting yourself to a religious cause instead.

Developing Emotional Sensitivity

For decades, people have debated whether human behavior and personality characteristics are more the result of genetics or experience.

The general overall belief—no surprise here—is that both your biology and your environment or life experiences contribute to your personality and your ability to manage your emotions.

As a therapist who practices and teaches dialectical behavior therapy (DBT), I base my views about emotional sensitivity on Marsha Linehan's Biosocial Model (1993). Linehan, a psychologist and the treatment creator of DBT, developed the Biosocial Model to explain the origin of borderline personality disorder (BPD). BPD is a disorder in which, basically, people have difficulty managing their emotions to the point they're emotionally unstable. Linehan's theory states that some people are naturally more emotionally sensitive than others; this sensitivity, combined with an environment that consistently invalidates these individuals as children—that is, tells them that they're wrong for the way they feel, think, or act—leads to the development of BPD.

In other words, your life experiences, including your family's actions and reactions and interactional styles, as well as those of other significant people in your life, either add to or lessen your difficulty in coping with intense emotions. This is not to say that if you're emotionally sensitive, you must have grown up in an invalidating environment. However, if your emotional sensitivity was not accepted and not understood in your family—perhaps your caretakers ignored your emotional sensitivity, or they reacted critically or even abusively—you may have particular difficulty accepting and managing your emotions.

The Hurricane Rating Scale of Emotional Sensitivity

Being emotionally sensitive and having difficult emotions doesn't mean you're fundamentally different from anyone else. Instead, think of being emotionally sensitive as living in a hurricane, whose strength varies according to how sensitive you are. At one end of the scale (category 1) are the individuals who are slightly more sensitive than the majority of people. These people experience noticeably increased emotional intensity but minimal damage to their relationships and life goals. Those in the middle of the scale (category 3) live with uncomfortable intensity and damage to the less stable parts of their lives, such as new relationships, business interactions, and any activity that produces anxiety (e.g., attending school). At the far end of the scale (category 5) are those who are the most emotionally sensitive, for whom emotions are consistently overwhelming and result in significant damage to most parts of their lives, including family relationships, friendships, and their ability to function on a daily basis.

It's vital that you have some idea of where you are on this scale, because if you live with category 4 or 5 emotional sensitivity (i.e., if you rated as "strongly emotionally sensitive" on the self-assessment in the introduction to this book) you'll need to be more active in using your coping skills than people who are less sensitive.

Psychological Disorders and Emotional Sensitivity

For reasons that are not clear, some people who are born with emotional sensitivity and have stressful life situations don't develop emotional, personality, or behavioral disorders, while others do. Some emotionally sensitive people have suggested that an intense interest, like reading, or a relationship with a supportive adult, such as a neighbor, parent, grandparent, or teacher, significantly improved their ability to adjust to life.

If you do have a diagnosis of depression, anxiety, BPD, or another disorder that reflects difficulty managing emotions, treatment of that diagnosis is of primary concern. There are at least nineteen studies showing that psychotherapy alters brain function in a positive way for people with major depression, post-traumatic stress disorder, obsessive-compulsive disorder, panic disorder, social anxiety disorder, specific phobias, and BPD (Rabinovitz 2012). Though this book isn't about treatment of these disorders, and isn't intended to replace therapy, the coping skills it teaches may still be beneficial to you. If you're currently in therapy, discuss the ideas presented in this book with your therapist before trying them. If you've completed therapy for an emotional disorder, the ideas in this book may be helpful in further reducing your emotional pain.

Putting It All Together

Being emotionally sensitive can be both your greatest gift and your greatest challenge. Sometimes it's difficult to appreciate the positives of emotional sensitivity, because experiencing emotions so intensely can be painful and lead to difficult situations. The next steps in learning to manage your feelings so that they don't overwhelm you are to look at how your sensitivity affects your life and to learn some basic emotion management skills.

CHAPTER 2

First Steps to Reclaiming Control

Logical thinking is often viewed as a sign of maturity and intelligence. If you're emotionally sensitive, wanting to live up to that standard of maturity and intelligence may add to your difficulty accepting and coping with your emotions, because your feelings often overwhelm your logic. Maybe you believe that life would be easier without sadness, jealousy, or fear—then you wouldn't have to endure the looks you get from others when you cry because you're angry, or then people wouldn't shake their heads as though you were a child when you wonder all day why your neighbor didn't say hello this morning. Life without emotions can sound quite appealing.

However, emotions provide important information for living your life in a safe and satisfying way. For example, fear tells you when to run from danger, love indicates whom to protect and form a relationship with, and joy enhances your capacity to appreciate positive experiences. Your emotions are also an important source of motivation. You don't want to waste time planning your escape when a hungry tiger is attacking you—you want to run. Emotion, not logic, motivates you to help the poor and others in trouble (Linehan 1993). Logic isn't the reason someone jumps into a freezing-cold lake to save a child from drowning. A good system for making everyday decisions, therefore, is to use logical thinking with input from your emotions.

Accepting your emotions and the information they convey can help you make better choices. Part of accepting your emotions is understanding the style in which you express them.

Types of Emotional Sensitivity

Emotional sensitivity can be evident in two very different ways: emotional reactivity and emotional avoidance. Although I'll describe these patterns of behavior separately, perhaps you go back and forth or are somewhere in the middle. Sometimes your behavior may depend on the situation.

Emotional Reactivity

If you tend to be emotionally reactive, you act on your feelings without thinking. You express anger, sadness, happiness, excitement, and other emotions with gusto. You'll jump on a plane to visit a friend even though you don't have the money to spare. You're the one who starts the line dances and sing-alongs at parties. If your boss doesn't approve your request for vacation, you'll send her an angry e-mail. If you find a text from a woman on your husband's phone, you might just throw all his clothes out onto the lawn. But the next day, when you're calmer and realize the note was innocent, you'll text him a hundred times to apologize.

When you're emotionally reactive, controlling the impulses that come with strong emotions is challenging. At the moment you write that angry e-mail to your boss, you don't care that you may be fired. When you dump your husband's clothes on the lawn, you don't consider there might be an explanation, such as the note was from his secretary about an appointment he had with a customer. At the time, your emotions tell you the action is right. But afterward you're embarrassed that you acted impulsively. You promise yourself, "Never again, never again," yet you always do it again.

For emotionally reactive people, a primary step toward decreasing chaos is to delay acting on urges. You need ways to calm your emotions so that you can think more clearly and decide what actions will be most effective. Mindfulness (see chapter 4) is an excellent way to develop a delay between the urge to do something and actually doing it. Calming techniques discussed later in this chapter will also be helpful.

Emotional Avoidance

If you tend to be emotionally avoidant, you don't want to face uncomfortable feelings or situations that cause them. Avoiding painful emotions altogether may seem like a good idea. You might numb your emotions through overexercising, overworking, overeating, and the like. Or you might push your feelings away so that you aren't aware of them, perhaps so quickly you don't even realize they occurred. Not feeling your emotions takes a lot of energy, so you're probably tired much of the time. In fact, a sudden feeling of tiredness may be a cue that you're pushing away emotions.

Maybe you're aware of your feelings but put on a mask for other people. You hold your smile in place and don't acknowledge even minor disappointments. You say things like, "I'm fine—everything is perfect." You may express anger to mask other feelings, such as sadness, that make you feel more vulnerable.

Mindfulness (see chapter 4) can increase your awareness of difficult emotions so that you can develop ways of coping with them. Taking steps to identify your emotions, such as analyzing your physical sensations, investigating your urges to act, and determining the cause (see chapter 5), will help you develop effective ways of responding to your emotions in which you act on the information that they provide (Linehan 1993).

If you tend to avoid your emotions, you may be particularly tempted to skip the exercises in this book. Instead, complete them carefully to help you not only learn the information but also overcome your avoidance.

CHASING GOOD FEELINGS

In general, emotional avoidance involves the pursuit of feeling good or avoiding pain in the short term, even when the long-term consequences are destructive. Avoiding difficult emotions by pursuing a feel-good agenda doesn't usually work. You may constantly chase happiness yet not find it. Think about how, after eating a cupcake, you may believe that eating another cupcake will be so wonderful. But the actual experience of eating a second dessert isn't likely to truly make you happy. You may drink more coffee, buy more clothes, and stand in line for a new phone, even though you already have all those things. A lot of craving and wanting actually results in unhappiness.

Overcoming your urges to overeat, overdrink, overspend, or otherwise attempt to feel good (and avoid difficult emotions) can be challenging. A first step is to have a plan for what you'll do when you have urges to engage in behavior that isn't helpful. Write out your plan. Find an effective replacement behavior such as exercise, playing games with friends, or calling friends for support.

Another option is to write out the many reasons to not engage in the behavior again. Keep that list with you, and read it when you're tempted to pursue those activities that actually add to your misery in the end. Some people carry an object such as a stone, a necklace with a symbol, or some other piece of jewelry to remind them of their commitment to not engage in false feel-good activities. If you find you're not able to stop, then consider seeking professional help or attending 12-step meetings.

Maybe part of your motivation to pursue good feelings is that you're scared of emotions. You may have developed a phobia of some or all of your emotions and become anxious at the first sign of feelings.

EMOTION PHOBIA

There are many reasons you may have developed a phobia of your feelings. Perhaps when you were younger, your caretakers punished you severely when you expressed a certain emotion, such as anger. You may have learned that having emotions is "wrong." Maybe you're fearful of sadness because you've suffered deep depression and fear that you'll relapse if you're sad. You may fear being out of control when you're emotional. Whatever the reason, you panic when you experience feared emotions. You may feel paralyzed or have the urge to flee at the first indication you're experiencing the emotions that scare you. Your panic may come on so quickly that you have no awareness of the emotion that triggered it and are aware only of being overwhelmed with anxiety.

Overcoming fear of your emotions necessitates letting yourself experience them. Only by experiencing them can you learn that they won't last forever and that you can tolerate them. Help from a therapist is likely to be important in this situation.

How Being Overwhelmed by Emotions Affects Your Life

Whether you tend to be emotionally reactive, emotionally avoidant, or sometimes one and sometimes the other, your feelings affect your life in many different ways. The following form will guide you in assessing the ways your intense feelings have helped and hindered you in different areas of your life.

You may find this exercise emotionally painful to complete. Have someone close by for support or make plans to do an activity after you've finished that will require your attention, such as having lunch with a friend or exercising. The activity should be one that can distract you from upsetting thoughts.

Identifying the reasons to change (in this case, to improve your coping skills) is a part of successful change. The emotions you may experience from doing the exercise will be temporary. However, if there's any unresolved trauma in your past, or if you have any reason to believe this exercise could greatly upset you, then do it only with the approval or help of a therapist.

The Cost and Benefits of Your Emotional Intensity

For each of the following categories, write the different ways being emotionally sensitive has both helped and hindered you. How your emotions have benefited you may not be immediately obvious, but if you think carefully, you'll probably find that your feelings have added to your life in significant ways. You can download a full-size version of this worksheet from http://www.newharbinger.com/29934.

Romantic Relationships, Marriage

How has being emotionally sensitive helped you in this area?

____

How has it hindered you?

____

Work

How has being emotionally sensitive helped you in this area?

____

How has it hindered you?

____

Parenting

How has being emotionally sensitive helped you in this area?

____

How has it hindered you?

____

Life Dreams

How has being emotionally sensitive helped you in this area?

____

How has it hindered you?

____

Friendships

How has being emotionally sensitive helped you in this area?

____

How has it hindered you?

____

Social Activities

How has being emotionally sensitive helped you in this area?

____

How has it hindered you?

____

Leisure Time, Hobbies

How has being emotionally sensitive helped you in this area?

___

How has it hindered you?

___

Spiritual Life

How has being emotionally sensitive helped you in this area?

___

How has it hindered you?

___

Now consider any patterns you notice in your answers. Do your intense emotions hinder you or benefit you in the same ways in each category? What exactly do you want to be different? For example, perhaps you frequently become discouraged and give up on projects you committed to completing, and you want to be able to follow through. Learning to cope effectively with discouragement would be one of your goals.

Next, you'll look at the specifics of how you express your emotions. Knowing your typical behaviors when you have certain emotions will help you communicate more clearly. Identifying your emotional response patterns can help you change the patterns that aren't effective or healthy.

Your Emotions and Behavior

Reproduce the following chart, or download it from http://www.newharbinger.com/29934. Over the next week or two, whenever you experience one of the emotions listed, first rate the intensity of the emotion on a scale of 1 to 5, where 1 = mild and 5 = very intense. Then write what you did when you felt that way. For example, if you felt sad, you may have cried. Or you may have talked with friends, overeaten, gone shopping, or pushed the feeling away.

Whatever you do with your emotions, you likely have expectations for what will happen. If you're sad, for example, depending on what you do, you may expect that you can avoid the sadness, not feel so alone, forget about what made you sad, find someone to pay attention to you, or even change the situation. If you overate when you were sad, maybe you focused on feeling better in the short run and ignored how you might feel in the long run. Write what you were expecting would happen when you did what you did.

In the column labeled "Actual Results," describe what actually happened, in both the short term and the long term. Things may have gone exactly as you expected, or they may have gone differently. For example, maybe you wanted or expected your friend to ask what was wrong when you withdrew in anger and what actually happened is that she ignored you.

Try to record all this information as soon as possible after the experience. The sooner you do it, the more accurate and helpful the information will be.

Emotion	Intensity (1–5)	What You Did	What You Were Expecting	Actual Results (Short/ Long Term)
Sadness				

Anger				
Jealousy				
Frustration				
Fear				
Love				
Shame				
Rejection				

When the chart is complete (or nearly complete), review what you wrote for each emotion. Notice patterns in how your emotions affect your behavior. Some behaviors may be effective at helping you get what you want, while others might hinder you in living your life the way you want to live it. Are you doing the same behavior repeatedly in response to a particular emotion even though it isn't helpful or effective and maybe even has unwanted results? Do your actions change at a certain level of emotional intensity?

Keep what you learned from the preceding exercises in mind as you learn more about general skills for managing your emotions. You can replace the behaviors that aren't working well for you with more skillful behaviors.

First Steps to Control: Emotional First Aid

You've probably noticed by now that when you're filled with emotion, you often don't behave in logical ways, and the results of your actions—at least in the long term—aren't pleasant. That's likely to be no surprise. Maybe you've promised yourself many times that you wouldn't be controlled by your emotions. You may believe the problem is lack of willpower to stick to what you said you were going to do. But everyone's willpower is limited—you only have so much. You may keep to your promise for a few hours or days, and then your emotions will overwhelm you again (Baumeister et al. 1998).

Willpower doesn't work. Using sheer willpower, avoiding your emotions, and chasing ways to feel better will make you more miserable and more overwhelmed in the long run (McGonigal 2012). Some of the strategies that *do* work you probably already know but aren't using. When you feel out of control of your actions, it's difficult to see that you can take steps that make a difference.

The following techniques will help you feel less overwhelmed in general. In later chapters, you'll learn more detailed strategies. Remember, just knowing the strategies doesn't work—it's critical that you practice and use them.

Identify the Cause

If you're emotionally sensitive, you often are unsure about the reasons for your emotions. You may sometimes find that you're depressed, scared, or angry but don't know why. If you can accurately identify what you're feeling and the cause, then you'll know better how to cope effectively (Linehan 1993). For example, if you're afraid because a snowstorm is coming, then stocking up on food and putting snow tires on your car are logical and constructive steps to take.

Taking appropriate action to solve or make a difference in the problem will help you manage the emotion. Sometimes, though, there's no action you can take. If you realize you're anxious because someone you love is having minor surgery tomorrow, then there's nothing you can do to change the situation, but you can be aware that the reason for your upset is time limited. Knowing that you'll only have to cope with that anxiety temporarily, you can find ways to comfort or distract yourself.

Now imagine that you're anxious but haven't thought about the reason. You go through your whole week feeling uncomfortable. Finally you consider what might be causing your discomfort. You realize that you haven't heard from the company where you applied for a job last week. This helps you put the emotion in perspective. You might smile and shake your head, realizing that while you want the job, it wouldn't be terrible if you didn't get it. In this case, identifying the reason for your emotion helps you manage the emotion in a different way.

Sometimes, emotionally sensitive people say the reason for their upset is that really awful things do happen in the world. For sure, this thought adds to their misery. But general ideas such as this one are often the *result* of feeling sad or hurt rather than the *cause*. Look for specific events that led to the global judgment. If you think your life is a mess, what was the most recent example of your life being a mess? Detailed, factual statements, such as "My mom said she was angry and fed up that I asked for rent money again," can help you find solutions to problems. General statements of misery, such as "My mom's a selfish jerk," will only lead you to feel overwhelmed and hopeless.

Connecting the Emotion with the Cause

Over the next week, notice whenever you experience a strong emotion. Each time, fill out the following form (which you can make copies of, or download from http://www.newharbinger.com/29934) to help you notice patterns.

Emotion you're experiencing: ______________________________

Event that triggered the emotion (be specific): ____________________

Can you solve or lessen the problem? Is there any action to take?

____

If the problem can't be easily solved but is time limited, how can you comfort or distract yourself?

____

After you've done this exercise for a week, you may find it a little easier to connect your emotions with their causes. When you know the cause of any particular emotion, you'll have a better idea of how to cope effectively.

Recognize That Your Feelings Aren't Necessarily Reality

When you're feeling happy and joyful, you tend to think positive thoughts and all may seem right with the world. When you're upset, you may not remember how good you felt before and be unable to believe that you may feel good again, even though nothing in your life has significantly changed. During those times, your thoughts are often pessimistic, and you may see all as hopeless (Linehan 1993). Thoughts like *I feel miserable because the world is a horrible place and my life is a mess* may be typical.

That's just the way the human brain works. You tend to see the world based on your emotions at a given moment. For emotionally sensitive people, this can create an emotional roller coaster ride where one day you're up and the next day you're down.

One way to let go of the belief that your misery is forever is to track your feelings. Keep a diary in which you write about your emotions and the events that happened each day. After a couple of months, go back and review what you've written. You'll notice that your outlook tends to change with your feelings. Recognizing that your thoughts often reflect your feelings and not necessarily the facts of your life can be helpful.

Don't Feed Painful Emotions

It may seem logical that managing difficult emotions, such as sadness, involves not doing things that add to those emotions or make them stronger. However, this is harder than it sounds. When you're depressed, you probably won't naturally choose to be around happy people who are laughing. You're likely to seek out others who are unhappy. If you're angry with someone, you may think of more reasons to be angry with that person, with the result that you stay angry longer. If you've just broken up with your romantic partner, you'll be drawn to sad songs about lost loves. The good news is there are many ways that you can keep yourself from making difficult emotions even more intense.

STOP THE REPLAY

When you're angry or scared or experiencing other uncomfortable emotions, you may replay over and over in your head whatever happened to make you feel that way. You may look for additional evidence to support the way you feel, maybe to justify your feelings. You may remember all the wrongs people have done to you, all the times when a particular person was hurtful, or all the mistakes you've made. This behavior is so common there's a term for it—"throwing in the kitchen sink." Making a list of past wrongs doesn't help resolve the current situation, however—it only makes you more upset.

One way to stop reigniting your emotions is to gently remind yourself to stay in the here and now. Focus only on the current situation, and if your mind goes to the past, gently refocus your attention—again and again, if you need to (see chapter 4 for more specifics).

You could also try the following informal mindfulness exercise: Notice your thoughts about past experiences that upset you. Then notice whether the thoughts are helpful. Describe the thoughts as such—say to yourself, *That's a helpful thought*, or *That thought isn't helpful.*

Another option is to practice acceptance (Linehan 1993). Accepting what happened doesn't mean that you approve of or agree with what happened. Accepting what happened means only that you acknowledge it occurred. You stop wishing it were different, believing it shouldn't have happened, or blaming others, and accept that it did happen and it's over. Acceptance is also about your thoughts. Accepting that you're having an upsetting thought means you stop fighting the thought. Each time you experience the thought, you label it—"That's a thought"—and stop yourself from going down the "what if" path. By doing so, you're recognizing that just because you think something doesn't mean it's true. Humans have thoughts all the time that don't reflect reality. Many of our thoughts are about things that are out of our control.

You can also substitute other thoughts in order to stop an unhelpful review of an upsetting situation. Counting backward from one hundred by threes or doing multiplication tables in your head, for example, could be helpful.

ABANDON EMOTIONAL REASONING

When your emotions are intense, it's easy to believe the thoughts that accompany them. These thoughts are called *emotional reasoning.* Sometimes just experiencing fear or another upsetting emotion leads you to be sure something awful must be happening or about to happen because of your feeling. For example, if you're afraid you'll fail your test, you may have the thought *I'm sure I'll fail my test.* Or if you fear something is seriously wrong with your health, you may think, *I must truly be ill.*

Believing such emotionally generated "facts" about what's going to happen or what did happen may make the situation worse. For example, if you buy into the thought *I'm sure I'll fail my test* based on the feeling you have, you may avoid taking the test or studying for it, because it seems pointless. Thus you forfeit or damage your chances of actually passing the test. If you believe the thought *I must truly be ill,* you may avoid seeing a doctor because you'd rather not know just how bad it is. If so, any medical problem you have could become more serious and difficult to treat. You also forgo the chance that the doctor would tell you you're not ill and thus end your constant worry.

Emotions provide you with information, but sometimes that information can be misinterpreted. Emotional reasoning can be like a false alarm. You may be worried about the outcome of your medical tests, but the emotion doesn't mean that the outcome is doomed. Feeling anxious about a job interview doesn't mean you aren't going to get the job.

Emotional reasoning is different from intuition. When you're using your intuition, there's a calm sense of knowing (Linehan 1993). You just know something is true, even though you can't articulate why, and there's little emotion associated with that knowing. When you're using emotional reasoning, you're often distressed and agitated.

Determining whether you're reacting to intuitive knowledge or emotional reasoning is important. If you're reacting to emotional reasoning, then acknowledge that your thoughts are based on your emotions and not on facts. Try the breathing exercises, the relaxation exercises, and the other ideas in this chapter to help reduce the uncomfortable feeling.

Take a Break

When you're experiencing an uncomfortable emotion, such as anger or fear, you probably want to settle the issue as soon as possible. Instead, practice taking a break until you're calm, so that your logical thinking can emerge. What you do during that break is important. Some actions will help you manage your emotions effectively, and other actions will increase your emotional upset. Here are some recommendations.

Breathing Exercises. Your body tends to be tense when you're emotionally upset. Simply slowing your exhalations is a way of calming yourself. One way to do this is to breathe out to a count of seven. Breathe in through your nose and out through your mouth, pursing your lips or puffing your cheeks and making a blowing sound. You can add to this exercise by counting while breathing in as well. Whatever number you use for breathing out, breathe in for half that number. For example, if you breathe out to a count of seven, breathe in for a count of three or four. Repeat four times. Practice once or twice a day, in addition to any time you're upset.

Visualization or Guided Imagery. Visualization is a way of coping by using your imagination to picture relaxing events. Guided visualization or guided imagery is when someone tells you what to picture, often in a video or audio recording. People often engage in visualization to reduce their tension or to help themselves stop going over and over upsetting events in their minds.

You might want to visualize all your difficulties being taken away. For example, picture your troubling thoughts being packed one by one into a steel case that you chain and lock. Then picture putting the case at the bottom of a deep hole and covering it with concrete. Or you might want to visualize being in a relaxing place, as in the following example.

Get in a comfortable position. Breathe deeply and slowly in and out. Continue this slow breathing. Feel the air enter your body, and feel it as you release it. As you release your breath, notice how the muscles in your face relax. Feel yourself getting heavier and heavier. At this moment in time, you have nowhere to go, nothing to do. Focus on your breath as you breathe in and out, relaxing your muscles.

Picture yourself walking toward a long, sandy beach. The sand is almost pure white, soft and warm under your bare feet. The air smells slightly salty and clean. As you get closer to the ocean, you notice the brilliant blue water is crystal clear. Shells of all shapes and sizes glisten on the shoreline or twinkle beneath the waves. You stand where you are for a few moments, just watching and listening to the gentle surf. The sun feels warm on your skin, and there's not a single cloud in the sky. A gentle breeze blows, leaving tiny drops of sea spray on your face and arms. Occasionally you hear the far-off high-pitched cry of a gull. After a while, you notice a grove of palm trees a short distance away, surrounded by tropical flowers. You walk over to smell the flowers and you discover a hammock strung between two of the palm trees. You climb into the hammock, resting your head on the pillow that's there. You lie still, listening to the waves coming in and going out, coming in and going out, over and over. You breathe in and out, letting go of all stress.

Create Your Own Visualization

Making visualization more personal can make it more effective. Maybe you prefer a cabin in the mountains to a beach. Perhaps certain smells or sounds are particularly comforting to you. To help you come up with ideas for your personalized visualization, follow these instructions, writing out your responses.

1. Describe your favorite way to relax.
2. Describe in detail your most relaxing things to see.

3. Describe in detail your most relaxing things to smell.
4. Describe in detail your most relaxing things to touch.
5. Describe in detail your most relaxing place. Include how you experience this place in terms of all your senses.
6. Describe in detail any people you want to include in your visualization.
7. Would you rather walk around or stay still in your visualization?

Now weave all the above together into a visualization narrative. If your favorite smell is apple pie, for example, you can have that smell float by you no matter where your favorite place is. Once you've written out your visualization, have a friend record it for you or record it yourself. Keep it on your phone or another device where you have ready access to it.

Progressive Muscle Relaxation. Progressive muscle relaxation reduces muscle tension and lowers your anxiety level. In this technique, basically, you tense groups of muscles as you breathe in, then relax them as you breathe out. You do this starting with the feet, say with your toes or calves, and work your way up to your face. Progressive muscle relaxation can help reduce anxiety, and helps with insomnia as well.

Distraction. Sometimes the best way to calm yourself is to distract yourself from whatever is upsetting you. Remember to let yourself feel whatever emotions are present before using distraction. Feeling the emotions is important so that you get the information your feelings are giving you and you aren't using distraction as avoidance. But continuing to feel intense emotions over hours can be exhausting, and you need to have ways to take breaks from the emotions when possible. Maybe you can play a game, watch a movie, or call a friend to chat about other topics. Of course, distraction won't eliminate the painful feelings, but it can help you tolerate them until the situation passes or your feelings decrease in intensity.

Reset. Sometimes it can be difficult to let a feeling go. Finding ways to "reset" yourself emotionally can help. The old saying that things will look better in the morning is often true (Cartwright 2010). If little else works, go to sleep if you can. You'll most likely wake up with less emotional upset.

Exercise is great for lowering your anxiety and calming your feelings so that you can think more clearly. Any exercise that increases your heart rate should work.

Changing your body temperature can also be helpful. Showering with cold water or going for a walk in chilly weather could be a good strategy.

Sometimes just laughing out loud—a long, deep belly laugh—will work to decrease your emotional anguish. If so, you can keep funny videos on hand, or just throw yourself into laughing.

Remember the Big Picture

Your emotions can blind you to facts about people or situations that don't support the emotions you're experiencing at the moment. When you're angry with someone, for example, it's unlikely you'll think of all the times that person was kind or helpful. Anger narrows your vision so that all you see is how horrible the other person is and how much you dislike him.

For example, let's say your wife forgot to get last-minute groceries that you need for a party you're hosting in an hour. Most likely you'll be angry and recall all the other times she hasn't come through, forgetting those times when she was helpful or kind. If you can push yourself to think of the times your spouse has been supportive, you'll have a more balanced and accurate view.

Consider writing a list of the ways the people in your life support you and help you. Keep the list handy. When you're feeling angry or upset with them, read the list to help you keep the "big picture" in mind.

Create a Different Emotion

Sometimes managing your emotions means creating a different emotion, one that's more pleasant. Particularly when an emotion is taking a long time to dissipate and the circumstances don't seem to fit with the intensity of your feelings (that is, you aren't sure why you're feeling this way), it would be good to engage in an activity that creates the opposite emotion to what you're feeling (Linehan 1993). If you're depressed or anxious, for example, it may be helpful to watch a show that makes you laugh. If you're angry, try watching a scary movie. Talking with or simply thinking about people you love (or who love you) may also work. Focusing on compassion toward someone you're angry with can also change your emotion.

Think Here and Now

Sometimes when you're overwhelmed with emotion, it's because you're thinking about the future. You may be wondering how you'll ever get a college degree when you're still taking freshman courses, or how you'll ever get moved into a new home when you've only just started looking. Maybe you're telling yourself there's no way you can get through the rest of the week.

To help you get some perspective on the situation, imagine how it would feel to a young child to think about reading a college textbook. You may be easily overwhelmed any time you think about the end goal. On the other hand, if you think just about what you need to do now, you can manage.

Maybe everyday events often lead you to have overwhelming thoughts and emotions, such as *How will I get through the day after that insult from my sister?* The answer is still the same: focus on your immediate next action. If your next task is to go to the grocery store, just focus on getting in the car, then focus on driving to the store, and then focus on each item on your grocery list. Doing only what you need to do in the moment will decrease your sense of being overwhelmed.

Let Yourself Cry

If you're emotionally sensitive, you may be particularly prone to tears. You also are likely to worry about what crying might mean about your character. Perhaps people tell you that you cry "all the time," and you judge yourself negatively as a result. You may see crying as a sign of weakness. Yet crying is actually a way of coping with strong emotions. There are good reasons to cry.

First, crying is considered a cooperative behavior—a behavior meant to facilitate peace and friendship rather than adversity. Crying signals to others that you don't want to fight. (After all, you can't really fight well with tears flowing from your eyes.)

Second, crying signals a willingness to be vulnerable in relationships, which is a necessary component of intimacy. Crying shows others that your walls are down and you're undefended. It's a profound opportunity for you and another person to grow closer. In this way, crying can help you build intimate relationships that will hopefully contribute to a life of contentment.

Third, crying is usually an effective means of obtaining help or comfort, as most people have an instinct to offer help or comfort to someone who's crying. In fact, crying is universally recognized as a sign of distress.

Fourth, crying is a way to express different emotions. People may laugh until they cry. They cry for joy as well as fear, sorrow, and sadness. Some people cry when they're angry. Sometimes you may find yourself crying due to overwhelming feelings you cannot put into words.

Finally, crying can help you calm yourself. Chemicals released in your tears as well as in your brain can help you feel better after crying (Frey 1985). Letting yourself cry can be a positive coping skill.

Practicing Emotional First Aid

Take a week to practice the skills discussed in this chapter. Practice when you're not upset, as well as when you are. Then write how you used each skill and summarize in what ways it worked or didn't work. You may find that practicing for several more weeks, while continuing to read this book, will help you strengthen your skills still further. You may also want to come back to this exercise (and others) after you've completed the book. You can enlarge the following worksheet (or download a full-size version from http://www.newharbinger.com/29934).

Identifying the Cause

How you used this skill: ______________________________

How it worked: ______________________________

Not Feeding Painful Emotions

How you used this skill: ______________________________

How it worked: ______________________________

Taking a Break

How you used this skill: ______________________________

How it worked: ______________________________

Remembering the Big Picture

How you used this skill: ______________________________

How it worked: ______________________________

Creating a Different Emotion

How you used this skill: ______________________________

How it worked: ______________________________

Thinking Here and Now

How you used this skill: ______________________________

How it worked: ______________________________

Letting Yourself Cry

How you used this skill: ______________________________

How it worked: ______________________________

Putting It All Together

Emotions can overwhelm your logic to the point that you act in ways that detour you from the life you want to lead. Paying attention to and understanding your emotional response patterns and how they affect your life may be uncomfortable, but it'll help you know what you need to do to manage your emotions. In this chapter, you learned some general coping strategies. In the chapter to come we'll get more specific about how to effectively manage your emotions.

CHAPTER 3

The Basics Make a Difference. Really.

You probably already know you should get enough sleep and exercise. You've probably heard it from your mother, from your doctor, in magazine articles, and in health news stories. But did you know that practicing these basic ideas, actually living them each day, can improve your ability to manage your emotions (Linehan 1993)? We all have less emotional control when we're sick, tired, or hungry. And if you're emotionally sensitive, you'll be overwhelmed by your emotions more than others would be under similar conditions, so it's especially important to take care of yourself.

Overwhelming emotions often get in the way of not only having a healthy daily routine, such as getting regular sleep and exercise, but also staying organized. Taking time to actually care for your physical health and organize your environment, not just intellectually understanding the importance of doing so, will improve your life more than you might imagine.

Sleep

Sufficient sleep helps your brain function more effectively in many ways.

First, the time you spend in sleep is the only chance for your *prefrontal cortex* to rest and recover. This area of your brain, right behind your forehead, is believed to help you maintain control of your emotions, analyze situations, and predict what's likely to happen if you take certain actions, such as quitting your job or accusing your friend of avoiding you. In other words, your prefrontal cortex does most of the difficult work of making good decisions. Whether you're resting on the beach, reading a good book, or listening to music, your prefrontal cortex is working (Randall 2012). It's always working away, except while you're sleeping.

Second, during sleep, your brain is able to find connections and make associations between ideas. If you have a problem that you don't know the answer to, after a good night's sleep you may arrive at the solution. Maybe you'll wake up with just the right word for the song you're writing or a clear idea of how to organize the carpool schedule.

Finally, sleep may contribute to a higher tolerance for irritations, better problem-solving skills, increased understanding of social cues, and mental flexibility. For example, you'll likely find you're more understanding of other people's views and better able to adapt to changes in your schedule if you got a good night's sleep (Randall 2012).

When You Don't Get a Good Night's Sleep

If you're emotionally sensitive, your feelings may make it difficult to get the rest you need. You may worry so much that you have difficulty falling asleep, wake up too early and can't go back to sleep, or wake up throughout the night.

Lack of sufficient sleep will mean you'll have even more difficulty managing your emotions and making effective decisions. You'll react faster and with more intense feelings to smaller issues when you're tired. When you don't sleep well or enough, you may experience memory problems, attention and concentration problems, and diminished problem-solving ability. You lose your ability to understand the meaning of new information, and your thinking becomes more rigid. Lack of sleep can decrease your sense of hope and optimism, and this can feel like depression. Your stress threshold is lower when you don't get enough sleep, so that even routine tasks may seem overwhelming and small irritations might balloon into big ones. Driving a half mile to the store for milk can seem like too much work. Effectively responding to your screaming children in the grocery store might seem impossible.

Cognitive flexibility, an important part of being resilient and able to bounce back from difficulties, seems to be partly dependent on sufficient sleep. *Cognitive flexibility* means that you're able to see different points of view and to change your thinking in response to new information and situations. For example, if you're upset that your husband was late getting home, you can change your view when you learn he was changing a tire for a friend. But when you're sleep deprived, you may stay stuck on being upset that he's late and be slow to adjust your reaction based on added facts (Randall 2012). That difficulty in adapting your thinking to new information will make it even easier to be overwhelmed by your emotions.

When you don't get enough sleep, you also lose your ability to self-assess—to determine whether something you're doing is helping solve a problem or making it worse (Randall 2012). For example, you might not realize that the reason your friend is becoming more and more upset even though you keep apologizing for something is because you're continuing to talk about whatever it is that upset him. It's also harder to understand someone else's viewpoint. For example, you may be unsympathetic to your teenage son's belief that his life will be ruined if you drive him to school. All these issues can increase the disagreements you have with those you love.

Improving Your Sleep

Solving your sleep problems won't be easy, but it'll likely have positive effects on both your emotional and your physical health. As with most problems, the solutions to sleep problems are not immediate but require gradual implementation, with the results becoming more evident over time. The significant improvements you'll gain in your ability to manage your emotions will be well worth your efforts.

CREATE A COMFORTABLE SLEEP ENVIRONMENT

Your surroundings may affect your sleep more than you realize. The following guidelines can help you make your bedroom more of a soothing retreat, so that with time you may look forward to being in your bed rather than dreading it as the place where you toss and turn every night.

The best environment for sleep depends on your preferences. Your bedroom may be more calming and conducive to sleep if it's decorated in a way that pleases you. In addition, a room that's organized and neat is likely to feel more relaxing than a messy one.

You'll likely prefer a calm environment, one that feels safe. The pictures, the furniture, the books—all the objects in the room should be emotionally neutral or have a connection to something positive. Remove anything that upsets you, makes you feel tense, or has a connection to something negative—such as a bed that belonged to a disliked family member.

If possible, designate your bedroom as a no-stress zone. Avoid doing any activities in your bedroom that might bring tension into that space, such as work or work-related activities. Once you begin using your bedroom only for resting and sleeping, your body and mind will soon come to understand that the bedroom is a place to relax.

Being physically comfortable is also important to getting a good night's sleep. As much as your budget will allow, invest in a mattress and pillows that fit your preferences. Try out different mattresses in a store to see what feels best to you.

Most people sleep best in a dark room. If you cannot keep light from entering your bedroom at night, try a sleep mask. You'll also sleep better if the temperature is comfortable for you. A good nighttime temperature for most people is between 65 and 72 degrees Fahrenheit. If your feet tend to get cold, maybe sleep in socks.

Some people sleep best with quiet, and others sleep more deeply with background noise, such as a radio or television at a low volume. Experiment with silence, quiet voices, and calming music to see what works best. You might try playing audiobooks, recordings of white noise, or recordings of rain, ocean waves, or other nature sounds to help you relax. Or you might prefer to wear earplugs.

EVENING ACTIVITIES AND ROUTINES

Engaging in soothing and calming activities for the hour or two before you go to bed can help you be ready for sleep. If you normally exercise late in the day, consider exercising earlier. Although exercise may make you feel tired, it's hard to actually fall asleep within a few hours of being physically active. Watching scary movies or upsetting programs, completing work or work-related tasks, and thinking about your problems may also make it harder to fall asleep. Even the news may trigger emotions that interfere with unwinding and relaxing. The light from television or computer screens might keep you awake longer too, even after you've turned them off. Instead, try reading a book or light magazine, listening to calming music, doing puzzles, or talking with family members. Dimming the lights half an hour or more before you retire and wearing loose, comfortable clothes can help you prepare for rest. If a shower or a bath tends to calm you, then that could be part of your bedtime routine. If not, then take care of nighttime hygiene, such as washing your face and brushing your teeth, thirty minutes or so before bedtime.

It can be helpful to do the same relaxing activities each evening. Your body will become accustomed to your routine, with the result that you'll feel sleepy after doing your evening activities. Going to sleep and getting up at the same time every day is also helpful for the same reason.

CALMING EMOTIONS AND THOUGHTS

Lying in bed unable to sleep can be an unpleasant experience. Maybe you get upset thinking about how tired you'll be in the morning. Maybe you have a particularly demanding day ahead and you worry you won't be able to perform your best. Maybe you think about how much you hate not sleeping. While understandable and natural, those thoughts and worries make getting to sleep even more difficult.

Accepting that you're not sleeping is an important step in decreasing your discomfort and the tension that makes it more difficult to sleep. Maybe you can change the thought *I hate this* to *I'm not able to sleep, and I wish that weren't true. I can still rest.* Try releasing muscle tension as well. Progressive muscle relaxation (see chapter 2), for example, reduces anxiety and helps your body relax.

Perhaps all your worries come flooding into your head when you lie down to sleep. If you're emotionally aroused or can't stop thinking about problems, then try visualization (see chapter 2). Next, occupy your mind with a task such as counting backward from one hundred by threes or thinking of a different zoo animal for each letter of the alphabet. Do the task mindfully (see chapter 4).

If you find that when you're in bed your thoughts race or you're thinking about worries, things you need to do, or ideas to put in action, try keeping a pen and paper by your bed so that you can write down whatever's on your mind. Sometimes it's helpful to write down a specific time when you'll focus on what's concerning you. For example, plan to give that problem you're consumed with your full attention at 10:00 a.m. the next day. This simple action often works well to help you let go of repetitive ideas. You may feel an instant relief and soon fall asleep.

A guided-imagery recording may help you focus your attention on a pleasant or relaxing experience instead of the worries or problems that are looping in your head. Listening to a voice guide you to imagine walking along a beautiful beach may work better than just visualizing it yourself. Having a friend or someone you love record a guided-imagery exercise for you may be even more effective.

LIMIT CAFFEINE AND ALCOHOL

For some people, drinking caffeine or alcohol after a certain time makes it difficult to fall asleep, to stay asleep through the night, or both. Some people who drink caffeine or alcohol have no trouble falling asleep but often wake up early and can't go back to sleep. If you're one of those whose difficulty isn't falling asleep but staying asleep, you may not realize the effect that caffeine and alcohol have on your body and your sleep—even when you consume them well before your bedtime. If you could use a better night's sleep, try decreasing the amount of alcohol and caffeine you consume for a week and see what happens.

ADDRESS MEDICAL CONCERNS

Talk with your physician about the sleep problems you're having. She may refer you to a specialist, who will assess you for sleep disorders such as sleep apnea, a common disorder in which you breathe shallowly or irregularly while you sleep. Not only does sleep apnea disrupt your rest, it can lead to serious health issues and is linked to depression.

Ask your physician whether any medications you're taking may interfere with your sleep, as some antidepressants are known to do this. Your doctor might change the medication, or perhaps have you take such medications in the morning instead of at night. Your doctor can also discuss other solutions with you, such as possibly adding a prescription sleep medication.

Over-the-counter sleep aids might also be helpful. Supplements of synthetic *melatonin*, a hormone that helps control your sleep-wake cycles, are generally considered safe when used in low doses. The supplement does have side effects, such as lowered body temperature, morning grogginess, small changes in blood pressure, and vivid dreams. These side effects go away if you stop taking the supplement.

MAKE A PLAN AND KEEP A SLEEP DIARY

A sleep diary is a record of your sleeping and waking times, with related information, such as activities you do before bed and how much caffeine you drink each day. Keeping a sleep diary for several weeks can help you identify ways to improve your sleep.

When you first start to keep a sleep diary, don't make any changes in your sleep routine. Take a week to simply gather information about your current habits. Record the number of hours you slept each night, as well as the time you went to bed and the time you woke up. Then write down exactly what changes you'll make to your bedroom, your activities and routines before bedtime, and your caffeine and alcohol intake (see suggestions above). Decide how you'll address any medical concerns you have and how you'll manage disruptive emotions and thoughts. Be specific. The example sleep diary below may serve as a guide in developing your sleep plan.

Once you've developed a sleep plan, follow it for four weeks. Keep a sleep diary for each of the four weeks. (You can follow the format below, or download a full-scale copy of it from http://www.newharbinger.com/29934.) You could add any other activities that you know are important to track, such as whether you took a bath or limited your television or computer time prior to going to sleep each night. The more closely you follow your plan, the more likely you'll get the results you want.

At the bottom of each column, record how many hours of sleep you got and how rested you feel when you wake up the next day, with 0 being the least restful you've ever felt and 5 being the most restful you've ever felt in the morning.

	Example	Mon	Tues	Wed	Thurs	Fri	Sat	Sun
Set Bedtime Routine	*Completed*							
Set Bed and Wake-up Times	*Yes*							
Early Exercise	*Yes*							
Light Dinner	*Salad with chicken*							
Amt. of Caffeine	*2 coffees*							
Amt. of Alcohol	*1 glass wine at 6*							
Soothing Activity Before Bed	*Reading*							
Calm Emotions	*Guided imagery*							
Dark Room	*Yes*							
Comfortable Temperature	*Yes*							
Keep Your Mind Busy with a Boring Task	*Didn't need*							
Visualization	*Yes*							
Write Recurring Thoughts	*Yes*							
Noise/Quiet	*White noise*							

Acceptance	*Yes*								
Hours Slept	8								
Restfulness on Waking (0–5)	4								

After four weeks, evaluate your results. Did you increase or improve your sleep at all? Maybe you noticed feeling more rested, having more energy during the day, not waking in the early morning, falling asleep more easily, or not experiencing an early afternoon slump. Four weeks isn't a long time to practice a new sleep routine, so if you detect positive changes but aren't yet getting sufficient sleep, keep filling out your sleep diary for another two weeks. If you still aren't getting enough sleep, talk with your doctor.

Exercise

Exercise is one of the best ways to keep intense emotions under control. Being physically active can help regulate your mood just as well as or even better than medication, for the following reasons:

- It serves as a distraction from things that are upsetting you.
- It reduces muscle tension.
- It increases and balances *serotonin*, *dopamine*, and *norepinephrine* (important neurotransmitters involved in mood).
- It improves resilience by showing you that you can be effective in controlling your emotions.
- It can break the experience of being trapped and helpless.

In addition to helping regulate your mood, exercise enhances your ability to learn. It improves your attention and your capacity to adapt and bounce back following a mistake. When you're practicing new coping skills, how well you process new information and recover from choices that don't work is obviously important.

Exercise also increases cognitive flexibility (Ratey 2008). As discussed earlier, cognitive flexibility is the ability to integrate new information into your understanding of a situation. This same ability also involves applying new problem-solving strategies and using information in creative ways.

Being physically active helps relieve and repair the effects of stress on your body. When you're stressed, your body produces *cortisol*, a hormone that puts you on high alert and mobilizes your body's resources to help you respond to immediate physical threats. Although much of our stress results from psychological threats, emotional threats, and worries about the future, our bodies respond just as if the threat were physical and immediate. When the threat is an actual physical one, you can decrease your cortisol by taking dramatic physical action, such as fighting or fleeing. When the threat is psychological, emotional, or imaginary, on the other hand, there's usually no such action you can take, and so your cortisol level remains high. As a result, it's hard to think clearly, because your body is primed for action, not rational thought—the tendency is to see potential threats everywhere. If you're under constant stress, overexposure to cortisol and other stress hormones can also disrupt your body's functioning and lead to heart disease, anxiety, depression, weight gain, sleep problems, and memory impairment.

Exercise can be quite effective in helping you manage overwhelming emotions. Some people notice lowered anxiety levels after six weeks of consistent cardio workouts. As well as your ability to concentrate and learn, your physical health can improve. You can also have fun, if you choose an activity you enjoy. In addition, other efforts to improve your ability to manage your emotions will work better if you exercise regularly.

Identifying what type of exercise activity might work best is important, because you're more likely to begin and continue an activity that fits your preferences and lifestyle.

Your Exercise Style

The following questions are designed to help you think more specifically about activities you'd be most likely to do. Write out your answers.

Are you more comfortable exercising by yourself or with friends?

____

____

Do you enjoy competition?

____

____

Do you want to have set activities, such as attending a dance class, or do you want variety? Are there activities you'd really like to learn, such as boxing or rock climbing?

____

____

Are you more likely to exercise first thing in the morning or in the early afternoon?

____

____

Would you prefer to work exercise into your daily routine and not use special equipment or scheduled times?

____

____

GOING IT ALONE

If you prefer to exercise alone, consider creating your own routine. Write out two or three lists of exercises that will take you about thirty minutes, and do them five days a week. You might include jumping jacks, toe touches, marching in place, jumping rope, or hula hooping. Fitness magazines, books, and videos often have workout routines that you can follow if you don't want to create your own. Yoga videos are a good option too. Or walking or biking around your neighborhood, in a park, or on a school track might appeal to you.

HARNESS YOUR COMPETITIVE SPIRIT

If you're motivated by competition, then you might want to join a team or league, such as for racquetball, bowling, or tennis. Maybe you'd prefer to challenge a friend to ninety days of exercise and see whether you both can complete the exercises you choose together. You may set up a competition with yourself: can you exercise more or walk a little further than you did last week?

JUST PART OF YOUR DAY

If you want to integrate exercise into your daily routine, there are many ways to do so. When you walk to check the mail, go back and forth a few times. Park far away from the entrance of your destination and walk fast from your car to the door. Take the stairs instead of an elevator. Lift your grocery bags up and down as you carry them to your car. When you watch television, do leg lifts and other exercises.

MAKE A PLAN AND FOLLOW IT

It's time to get moving. So what are you going to do? Write down your plan for the next week, either on the chart that follows or on the form available for download at http://www.newharbinger.com

/29934. The more specific you can be, the more likely it is you'll follow through with the activity. Stating that you'll "go to the gym today at 9:00 a.m. and walk on the treadmill for fifteen minutes" is better than stating you're going to "start exercising."

Carry this plan with you—perhaps using a tracking application for your smartphone to measure your progress implementing it. Or you might post your plan on your refrigerator so that you can remind yourself to stick with it, and chart your progress. Tracking your new behavior will help you follow through and form a healthy new habit.

	Exercise	**Time Spent**
Monday		
Tuesday		
Wednesday		
Thursday		
Friday		
Saturday		
Sunday		

Find a way to keep yourself motivated. Visualize how much your fitness level will improve in three months. Reward yourself for each week you successfully follow your plan. Give yourself a treat, like a cup of your favorite tea or watching an episode of your favorite television show, after you exercise.

If you become discouraged, remember that starting any new habit can be difficult. When you first begin exercising, you may notice how out of shape you are. In fact, you may have been avoiding exercise partly to not have to confront that truth. Being a beginner at any activity is humbling and sometimes embarrassing. In addition, when you first start exercising, being physically active doesn't feel good: your muscles will ache and you'll wish you were on your couch relaxing. There are so many reasons and excuses you could list to not exercise. Just remember the benefits you'll gain by exercising regularly, even if you only walk around the block or lift a bottle of detergent ten times with each hand. You can do it!

Structuring Your Time

Emotionally sensitive people often say that having structure in their day, such as scheduled times to do certain activities, helps them accomplish tasks. That's partly because a commitment to do something at a certain time is more difficult to ignore than a vague "I'll do it soon." Accomplishing a necessary task usually is emotionally satisfying (or relieving) and helps you avoid the panic that results from waiting until the last minute. When you have appointments to keep, classes to attend, activities to do, and people to meet, you're also less likely to be focused on your emotions. As a result, those emotions won't seem so intense and may pass more easily.

You may be the kind of person who thrives when you've planned each hour of your day, or you may be the kind of person who feels overwhelmed by detailed planning. In addition, you may have a tendency to either underestimate or overestimate how long it'll take you to do things and how much you can do in a day. Perhaps the restrictions and pressure of a tight schedule increase your stress more than they help. When you try to do more than you have time for, you may find you don't have time to do necessary tasks. On the other hand, having too little to do can contribute to lethargy, sadness, or the belief that you have nothing to contribute. For all of these reasons, finding the right amount of structure will require trial and error.

Find the Right Amount of Structure

Set up a detailed schedule, one that includes many daily activities both at home and outside the home. Try following that schedule for a week. Then set up a second schedule that has just a few things to do each day. Use that schedule for a week.

If you don't work outside the home, your first schedule might look like this:

- *9:00 Wake up, eat breakfast, review schedule*
- *10:00 Exercise*
- *11:00 Shower and dress*
- *11:30 Necessary tasks (shop for groceries, clean the house, pay bills, etc.)*
- *1:30 Lunch*
- *2:00 Volunteer, apply for jobs, study for school, read*
- *3:00 Creative activity (write, paint, make jewelry, cook, work in the garden)*
- *4:00 Contact friends, visit neighbors, call family*
- *6:00 Dinner*

Your second schedule could have set times for two or three tasks or just a short list of what you'll do, with no times specified.

After you've followed each type of schedule for a week, evaluate your experience. Which type of schedule worked better?

Following a schedule may be challenging, yet it'll help you make decisions about time commitments. If you found you were too busy, then you may need to drop some activities. On the other hand, perhaps you found you needed more on your schedule.

Paying Attention to Your Environment

Emotionally sensitive people are often particularly reactive to their surroundings. You may not be comfortable in crowds or may dislike small, enclosed spaces. A messy or cluttered room may make you feel irritable, increase your negative thoughts about yourself, and contribute to overwhelming emotions.

Let's say there are dirty dishes piled in your kitchen sink, empty glasses left sitting around your living room, and papers and books on all the floors. Clothes are strewn on all the furniture in your bedroom. What message does this send to you? What emotions are you likely to experience in this type of setting?

If a messy room bothers you, perhaps one reason is that, for you, the mess reflects a lack of self-value. Another possibility is that the state of your home tells you that you're out of control or can't manage your life. Maybe the mess in your house reflects a sense of apathy or powerlessness. For any of these reasons, seeing your home a mess every day may influence the way you think about yourself. In addition, a messy house may add to your isolation, if you won't invite people over when your house is in disarray.

Wait a minute, you might be thinking. *My house is a mess* because *I've been sad, depressed, scared, or overwhelmed. My house is a mess* because *I think I'm helpless. My house is a mess* because *I'm emotionally sensitive and managing my emotions takes all my energy.*

That may be true. The problem is that having a cluttered or unkempt home could add to your down mood, lack of self-respect, thoughts of helplessness, thoughts of being overwhelmed, and lethargy. And, as in many situations, the problem spirals.

If your house is messy, you may be giving yourself the message that "messy" behavior is okay (Wilson 2011). Imagine you're sitting in your living room watching a movie on television, eating the last of the ice cream from the carton, and enjoying popcorn. There are papers everywhere, empty soda cans and candy wrappers on the floor, and unpaid bills scattered over the coffee table. When the movie is over, it's late and you feel lethargic from the junk food.

What are the chances that you'll put your spoon in the dishwasher, throw away the ice cream carton, and put away the uneaten popcorn? What are the chances you'll pay the bills?

If your house was clean and neat, the chances are higher you'd clean up after yourself and pay the bills. Even if you didn't do it that night, you'd be more likely to do it the next day.

Consider making small changes that will make your home pleasant and meaningful. You might want to clean for ten minutes each day in one room. Maybe start with your bedroom, where you wake up every day. Maybe you could clean for ten minutes in the morning and ten minutes at night. A different strategy would be to do one task each day. For example, on Monday you wash a load of clothes. On Tuesday you wash dishes. If you have too many possessions, then consider sorting through them. Keep the things that matter to you and give away the rest.

Keep the plan doable and simple. Track your progress. Reward yourself for each step that you take.

Putting It All Together

In my experience, taking care of your physical health, structuring your time, and organizing your environment are among the most important steps people can take to manage their emotions and create a sense of well-being. Yet working on getting better sleep, getting more exercise, and getting more organized is difficult, and you may doubt the importance of doing these things. If you're thinking, *Surely there's some new therapy or medication that will make more of a difference*, I suggest you conduct an experiment: put the changes discussed in this chapter into place, and judge for yourself the differences they make in your life.

CHAPTER 4

Introduction to Mindfulness

Mindfulness, a part of many psychological therapies, is a simple concept to understand, though not so easy to put into practice.

Jon Kabat-Zinn (1991, 4) defines mindfulness as "paying attention in a particular way: on purpose, in the present moment, and nonjudgmentally." This means keeping your mind in the here and now. For example, if you're eating dinner with your husband mindfully, then your attention is on your husband—that is, if that's where you want your attention to be (that's the "on purpose" part of the definition). You're also focusing only on what you can observe, without interpreting or judging. To continue the example, you might notice that your husband is smiling as he talks. That would be an observation. Thinking that he's a jerk would be a judgment.

Being able to focus your attention on what you observe is an amazing skill that can greatly affect your sense of well-being. Once you begin working on keeping your thoughts on the here and now, you'll be calmer and less stressed.

However, people in general aren't naturally mindful. Our thoughts tend to jump from one topic to another, often in an unfocused way. Our minds often wander into the past, ruminating over negative events we are powerless to change; or into the future, worrying over negative events that haven't even happened. If you're emotionally sensitive, your thoughts and intense emotions may often make it especially difficult to be "in the moment." You're more likely to be self-conscious and on guard, hyperalert to possible emotional threats. Training your mind to focus on the here and now will take practice, but the results will be worth the effort.

You can be mindful both of whatever is outside of you, like people, objects, or sounds, and of your internal experience—your thoughts, sensations, and emotions. Mindfulness of your internal experience will help you step back from your emotions rather than be engulfed by them. It'll give you a pause between your emotions and thoughts and your (re)actions, so that you can make thoughtful decisions. Whenever you can be mindful, you won't be lost in worries about the future or sadness about the past. You'll be accepting of yourself and others. Your emotions won't be able to take control.

Despite the advantages of being mindful of your internal experience, you may be hesitant to be more aware of your emotions, especially the painful ones. Yet being mindful of your emotions is an important skill.

Mindfulness of All Emotions

It's easy to believe that the presence of difficult emotions, such as sadness and hurt, means you must be doing something wrong. It may seem other people are happy most of the time; and when they do have problems, they solve them quickly and easily. A character on a TV show, for example, may seem able to resolve almost any dilemma by the end of the episode. Popular books and movies also perpetuate the myth of the happy ending, even when characters face overwhelming difficulties. Commercials would have you believe that you can be happy if you drive the right car or use the right deodorant. People in your life may seem to think that you could be better off if only you'd follow their simple advice—for example, to get a job, to get a backbone, or to stop being so upset. All of these influences may lead you to think that others can easily overcome the sort of problems you continually struggle with, meaning you're less capable than they are. If you're emotionally sensitive, you may already dread the intense pain of difficult emotions, and the idea that feeling sad or lonely makes you not normal, a failure, or even "crazy" only adds to your reluctance to experience any emotions other than pleasant ones.

Everyone is sad, lonely, angry, and hurt at times. Real-life problems are frequently not easy to solve, and it may take a long time for things to improve. Comparing yourself to others who you think have it better than you or pursuing material goods to make yourself feel better usually creates more misery.

If Only...Then I'd Be Happy

You may imagine that happiness is the result of achieving goals and gaining possessions. You may believe that you'll be happy when you have more money, when you get that promotion, or when you become a parent. Or you may think, *If I could just find someone to love, then I'll know joy*. The problem is that when you look to the future for happiness, you cannot be at peace in the present. Even when you obtain what you wish for, there's always something more to obtain.

You may believe that to be happy, you need to think and behave as others do. Thus, you look to others for how to live your life. If you can do what they do, you think, then you can be happy; then you'll be living life the "right" way. This typically leads to comparisons to others—usually people you believe are doing better than you. Perhaps you compare yourself career-wise to someone at the top of your profession or the most successful person that you know. You might compare your fitness level to that of a colleague who works out daily. Comparing yourself to the best attributes of others is likely to increase your discontent.

Being mindful entails living in the present moment and not judging yourself, your experiences, your emotions or other people.

Practicing mindfulness will help you stop the misery that comes from comparing yourself to those you believe are happier than you and judging your emotional experience.

Finding a Balance

Sometimes your thoughts may be all negative. For example, maybe it seems your life is one big struggle, while others' lives are all joy. This makes you feel sad and resentful. Or perhaps you focus on only one way that you can see yourself being happy, such as getting into a certain school or being married by a certain date. This may lead to feeling hopeless if you can't do these things.

Thinking that happiness is an either/or proposition—either you're happy or you're not—is like painting the complex and varied picture of your life in only one color. It can lead you to get caught up in negativity: if any part of your life is difficult, you may become upset, focusing only on the difficulty. For example, if someone speaks to you rudely in the airport, you find it impossible to enjoy the first hours of your vacation.

Being aware of the full truth of situations you're experiencing will help you balance your emotions, so that you don't suffer unnecessarily. If you tend to focus on or be aware only of difficulties, work on remembering the positive. List both the positives and the negatives of a situation, and weigh them in terms of their true importance. Then focus on the details of the positive experiences. Give your full attention to reviewing those positives multiple times. This process can help you see the whole rather than overfocusing on the negative.

You likely have either/or expectations in anticipating events as well. Imagine that you receive an invitation to lunch from a friend you haven't seen in a while. You can't wait to see him. The day you're supposed to meet him, you feel eager anticipation. Then you remember that the last time you met for lunch he told you about how well his job was going and about the new home he bought. You compared yourself to him, then judged yourself for not doing as well. You remember that this happens repeatedly whenever you see this friend. Now, instead of being excited to see your friend, you wish you hadn't agreed to meet him. You go from seeing only the positive to experiencing only the negative.

Being mindful of all the components of your relationships will help you balance your emotions. In the above example, awareness of both your excitement to see your friend and your tendency to compare yourself to him will help you stay balanced. Being mindful of the whole picture before you see him will give you an opportunity to prepare by letting go of your self-judgments.

If you can be not only mindful of the positive when you're upset, but also mindful of the *less* positive aspects of a situation when you're having a strong *positive* emotion, you can decrease your emotional ups and downs.

Being Aware of More than One Emotion

Being mindful of all the emotions you're experiencing means paying attention to those emotions that are less intense as well as those that are more intense. Though one emotion may seem to dominate at any one time, we often experience many different feelings at once. For example, you may be happy about finding a new job in another state, but sad that it means moving and leaving good friends. You may also be a bit scared of the challenge of moving, as well as hurt by someone saying you were bragging about your good fortune. If you focus on only one of those feelings, you'll lose information and emotional balance. When you're aware of one emotion, ask yourself what else is there—look for other emotions that might also be present.

Develop a Pause

Thinking before you act requires that you pause between noticing your thoughts and feelings and deciding what you'll do and say.

Perhaps that seems impossible because you've been acting on your emotions for years. Even so, through mindfulness, you can practice being aware of your internal experience, so that you're able to observe it without being completely caught up in it. You'll be able to say, "That's anger," or "That hurt," without acting on those feelings.

Think of how often you regret actions you took when you were emotional, and how much it might help if you could do this even just a little less often. With mindfulness, whenever you experience an emotional storm, rather than getting swept off your feet or charging ahead blindly through the pouring rain, you can observe the storm and wait until your mind becomes clear again so that you can think before acting.

When you practice awareness of your emotional experience and observing and accepting reality as it is, without judgment or interpretation, your emotions will be moderated and you can manage them more effectively. The benefits are many. Yet starting and maintaining a mindfulness practice is a challenge.

Practicing Mindfulness

You don't need to meditate to practice mindfulness. Usually, the best way to start practicing mindfulness is to be mindful of objects and actions.

Mindfulness of Objects

Being mindful of objects means focusing your attention on something outside of yourself. You can practice this at any time, as there are always objects around to focus on. You might try the following exercise at a time when you feel overwhelmed by your thoughts or emotions.

Mindfulness of Everyday Objects

Choose any object in the room—it doesn't matter what it is. For three minutes, focus exclusively on that object. Really see it. For example, if you're mindful of a pencil, you might notice its texture and ridges, its shape, how worn or sharp it is, its colors, how it feels in your hand, and how thick it is.

You may notice that while you're trying to maintain your focus on the object, your thoughts jump around to other things. You may think about your children, filing your taxes, the work project that needs to be done, your friend who's sick, and the guests coming for dinner tomorrow. This lack of focus can be discouraging. You may think you aren't doing the practice correctly. Recovering from distractions is a normal part of mindfulness, however. If you're frequently distracted, it doesn't mean mindfulness won't work or you can't do it right. When you become aware of a distraction, acknowledge it and gently bring your attention back to the object in the room.

In the beginning, you may find it helpful to have a set time or activity for practicing mindfulness. You might practice mindfulness while doing simple, everyday activities. You could choose to be mindful when you first wake up, maybe by focusing on the early morning sounds in your house. You could practice mindfulness when you're brushing your teeth, by focusing only on brushing your teeth: feeling the toothpaste in your mouth and the sensation of the brush bristles on your gums. Observe what there is to observe about brushing your teeth, without judging. You might notice that you judge your appearance as you look in the mirror, or you might think being mindful of brushing your teeth is silly. When you find yourself judging or your attention wandering, gently bring your attention back to whatever you're doing.

Sometimes, while you're practicing mindfulness, you'll notice an emotion arising. Don't ignore the emotion, but don't let it take over your attention either. Instead, try to gently be aware of the emotion as part of your experience. Name the emotion. Say to yourself, for example, *I have sadness*. Sometimes just acknowledging the emotion in this way will help loosen its grip on your attention. On the other hand, you might choose to be mindful of the sadness, particularly if you haven't been aware of being sad. You might notice where exactly you feel it in your body and what thoughts you have. You might be aware of what has triggered the sadness. On the other hand, if you're well aware of your sadness, know the reason for it, and have spent time expressing it, you might be better served by acknowledging the emotion and then gently bringing your focus back to whatever you're doing (e.g., brushing your teeth).

To stay mindful of an activity when emotions are distracting you, try breathing deeply and naming the emotion, as suggested above. If the emotion has no relevance to the present moment, you may want to point that out to yourself. For example, if you're sad about something that happened in the past, you might say to yourself, *That was sad. But that was then, and this is now.* If you're worried about the future in some way, you might say to yourself *That's a scary thought, but that thought isn't true now.* Acknowledge the emotion, and bring your focus back to the present moment. You may need to do this repeatedly.

Practice mindfulness on a daily basis, regardless of how your day is going or what emotions you're experiencing. If it seems your day is too busy for you to practice mindfulness, that's the perfect day to practice. You can be mindful even when you're in a hurry. If you move quickly but mindfully, you'll likely be even more effective at whatever you're doing, because you'll be less distracted.

Keeping track of your mindfulness practice will help you make it a part of your routine. Having mindfulness be a part of your regular daily activities—for example, making it a habit to be mindful whenever you're driving—is a good way to integrate mindfulness into your life.

Tracking Your Mindfulness Practice

Keep track of your mindfulness practice for one week. In the following spaces (or in a journal or notebook), write what you did mindfully each day. Download additional copies of this worksheet, if you need them, at http://www.newharbinger.com/29934.

Day 1: ______________________________

Day 2: ______________________________

Day 3: ______________________________

Day 4: ______________________________

Day 5: ______________________________

Day 6: ______________________________

Day 7: ______________________________

Now describe your experience. What did you notice about being mindful?

____

____

____

Think about how you can integrate mindfulness even further into your daily life. Perhaps you'll continue to be mindful at a certain time of day or while doing a particular activity. Write down your ideas.

____

____

____

Mindfulness of Emotions and Thoughts

Strong emotions scream for your attention, which is why pushing them away doesn't work in the long run. When you push your emotions out of your awareness because you don't want to deal with what caused them, they may come back later, triggered by something else. For example, maybe an incident at work makes you angry at your boss, but you don't acknowledge your anger because you're fearful of being fired. When you come home, you yell at your son for not picking up his clothes. You may be unhappy about your son's messy room, but the main cause of your anger was the incident at work.

When you're mindful of your emotions, you can notice the feeling and let it pass. Being mindful of emotions may initially increase their intensity, which can be uncomfortable, so begin by being mindful of emotions that aren't too difficult to manage. First, observe the feeling. The emotion will build, and you may fear that if you continue to give it your attention, it won't relent. However, if you turn away from the emotion while it's building, you won't learn through experience that the emotion will eventually peak and then dissipate on its own. So stay with the emotion, just notice it, and let it pass. Remind yourself that it's just an emotion. Emotions last only a short time if you don't push them away or build them up. When you're mindful of how you're feeling, the emotion that was screaming for your attention will feel heard and can then be quiet.

Being mindful of your emotions can be difficult to do on your own. You may wish to seek help from a therapist to learn mindfulness of your emotions. Not all therapists are trained in mindfulness techniques, however, so be sure to ask.

WORRY THOUGHTS AND ANXIETY

Many emotionally sensitive people are worriers. Worrying may seem to help you avoid bad events or prevent you from being caught off guard. Perhaps you consider your habit of worrying the price you pay to be prepared for negative events.

Although the events people worry about do sometimes happen, we truly don't know what the future will bring. Worry and anxiety about the future are therefore ineffective. In other words, they're simply not worth their emotional cost. In addition, when you worry, your mind isn't in the present moment. You're less able to focus on what's happening now, because you're busy thinking about events that haven't occurred. Instead of worrying, practice being mindful of your thoughts, accepting that you have worries, and bringing your mind back to the present without judging yourself. With time, you'll find that you can stay in the present or bring yourself back to the present more easily and decrease your worry thoughts.

MINDFULNESS AND THE WISH TO CONTROL

Emotionally sensitive people, in particular, often wish to control what happens in their lives as a way to avoid being hurt. Perhaps you plan, organize, and schedule your days in minute detail in an effort to make life predictable. Maybe you rehearse what you'll say in conversations. Perhaps you elicit promises from others as a way of trying to have control. Maybe you ask lots of questions to seek reassurance that people aren't upset with you or that they're not going to drop their relationship with you.

Facing your fears and being mindful of what scares you—such as change, uncertainty, and the emotions that come with those experiences—can be a challenge. Mindfulness of your fears and your attempts at control will again be helpful in letting go of behaviors that aren't effective ways of coping with your emotions in the long term.

Identifying Your Efforts to Control What You Cannot Control

As you go through your day, notice any time you experience a sense of anxiety and/or thoughts that you want something to be a certain way.

On a piece of paper (e.g., in a journal or notebook), record the following information:

- *The situation*
- *Your degree of anxiety*
- *Your thoughts about the situation*
- *What you're trying to control*

Repeat this activity for three days. When you have three days' worth of information, think about the situations you wrote down. See what patterns you can identify. Do you typically feel anxious about whether someone will like you or be angry with you? Do you have a pattern of attempting to control the emotions or thoughts that others have about you? Perhaps you typically attempt to control the choices or emotions of someone you love. In the future, try to approach those situations in a mindful way. Mindfulness involves acceptance of whatever you experience, including uncomfortable feelings. Accepting your feelings includes not acting in ineffective ways to reduce those feelings.

Mindfulness is an antidote to both avoidance and efforts to control. Whenever you practice mindfulness, you're working on your capacity to accept reality (including change and uncertainty), which will decrease your emotional suffering.

WAIT

Whenever you're upset and have an urge to act on your emotions, the following steps can help you decide on the most effective course of action.

Watch the emotion. Step back and observe your experience of the emotion. Be mindful of how the emotion feels in your body, what triggered the emotion, your thoughts about the emotion and/or the situation, and any urges you have. The emotion may ebb and flow, getting stronger before it gradually decreases in strength.

Accept that you're having an emotion, perhaps one you don't want to have. Acceptance means letting the emotion happen while recognizing that you don't have to act on it. Although sometimes you may feel controlled by your emotions, you don't have to be. Often no action is necessary.

If you're emotionally sensitive, it's likely that you have an urge to do something that will help you be *rid* of the emotion. Whatever it may be, this action may have become a pattern in your life. For example, perhaps you repeatedly seek reassurance from others that they still care about you as a way of trying to ward off sadness or fear of loss. Acceptance means letting the emotion happen while recognizing that you don't have to act on it *or* against it—efforts to control your emotions by resisting or attempting to get rid of them are just another way of allowing your emotions to control you, because you're still letting them dictate your behavior. Instead, know that it's okay to just feel whatever you feel.

Investigate. What information does the emotion give you? If you're angry about work, perhaps your anger is telling you it's time to look for a new job. Searching for the information your emotions provide can lead to effective actions that will help you move forward in your life.

Take time. Know that with time the emotion will pass. Let it. If possible, don't take any action until you're calmer, so that you can think through your actions more clearly.

Practicing WAIT

Practice WAIT (Watch, Accept, Investigate, Take time) and answer the following questions about your experience. You can do this multiple times, using copies of the following worksheet (available at http://www.newharbinger.com/29934).

Watch the emotion: What did you observe about your experience?

____

____

Accept the emotion: What was it like to accept the emotion? Did you have urges to stop the emotion in some way?

____

____

Investigate the emotion: What information did your emotion give you?

____

____

Take time: How were your thoughts about what action to take different after the emotion passed?

____

____

Know and Trust Your Internal Experience

Mindfulness of your internal experience (thoughts and feelings in particular) will allow you to know what you're feeling and to not act on your emotions impulsively. When you're able to label and manage your emotions effectively and think wisely, you'll learn to trust your thoughts, your decisions, and your emotional experience. You'll have a better sense of your identity.

Many emotionally sensitive people find they suffer from contagious emotions: they "catch" others' emotions. Any time you're with someone who's upset, you may become upset too. When the emotion calms, you may be confused by why you felt that way, because it didn't really fit with your beliefs or what was happening with you. Mindfulness will give you the opportunity to pause so that you can identify what part of your emotional experience, if any, is not your own. Pause, and be mindful—first of what emotions you're having, and then of why you're having them. If you realize you're upset because someone else was upset, then that information will help you cope with the emotions.

Mindfulness of emotions is a first step in accurately identifying your internal experience, which will help you trust yourself instead of depending on others to label your emotions and what thoughts you should have. Eventually, your relationships will likely be less rocky, because you won't be so fearful of people leaving you. You'll have more calmness, self-acceptance, and self-compassion.

Everyday Mindfulness

Practicing mindfulness of your emotions on an everyday basis will help you learn to be mindful more automatically. If you're emotionally sensitive, no doubt you'll have many opportunities on any given day to practice mindfulness of your emotions.

Mindfulness in Relationships

One example of using mindfulness on an everyday basis is being mindful of your responses to others. Imagine that your husband comes home without some item you asked him to pick up from the store. You get angry. You don't give him a chance to explain, because you don't want to hear some lame excuse. You already know the reason: *He must think I'm not important enough for him to remember what I asked.*

Yet your assumption may be wrong. What if, instead, you used mindfulness in this situation? If you were mindful, you'd notice that your husband didn't complete the errand you asked him to, but you wouldn't interpret this behavior or assume that it means anything. You'd accept that you couldn't know his motives. Perhaps he was too busy or too tired. Perhaps there were circumstances beyond his control—for example, the store was out of what you wanted.

The next time you find yourself making assumptions about someone's actions or intentions, be mindful of what you're doing. Practice WAIT. Remember to ask what happened and listen to the facts. Doing so will prevent unnecessary hurt feelings and damage to your relationships.

Mindfulness of Joy

Recognizing the joy there is in your life—your successes and the happy times—will help you cope with the hard times. Noticing only the hard times, on the other hand, can wear you down and contribute to feeling hopeless (Linehan 1993).

To practice being mindful of joy, make a list of all the positive experiences you've had in the last six months. Perhaps you can look back over a calendar, your blog, or your posts on social networking sites to help you remember. You may be surprised at how many positive experiences you've almost forgotten. Read your list weekly, and add to it as you can.

Purposefully doing enjoyable activities is a way of rejuvenating yourself and building your ability to cope with stress. Here's an informal exercise you might like to turn into a habit: Every day for the next week, do something that you enjoy, being mindful of your experience. Mindfully drink a cup of excellent coffee. Mindfully celebrate a birthday. Go to a beautiful garden and leave your phone and camera at home so that you can focus your full attention on what you see and smell, taking your time and walking slowly.

Mindfulness of Location and Activity

Being mindful of location and activity means being focused on wherever you are and whatever activity you're doing in the moment. So when you're at work, be mindful of your work. Focus your attention on one work task at a time. Then when you're at home, be at home. Leave work at work. When you're at worship, be at worship. When you're driving, be in the car and only drive. When you do one thing at a time, you'll lower your stress level, and that will increase your ability to manage your emotions.

Indicators That You're Not Being Mindful

Living each day in a mindful way will decrease your overall stress (Siegel 2010). That's not to say it's easy, even for those who practice mindfulness often. Being mindful as you go about your daily routine can be challenging. One of the most challenging aspects of mindfulness, particularly for emotionally sensitive people, is accepting reality as it is. Be on the lookout for the following indicators that you aren't being mindful. When you catch yourself doing these things, you can gently remind yourself to practice mindfulness.

Wishing

We all make wishes. Some wishes are small. For example, you may wake up one day and say, "I wish I didn't have to go to work today." You may stay in bed that morning longer than planned and then wish you didn't have to rush to get to work on time. You may finally walk into your closet and wish you had an outfit that fit and then wish you could lose ten pounds. Other wishes are big. For example, many people wish at times that their life situation was different.

We all make wishes, but wishing can keep you unhappy. Wishing can block taking effective action, such as accepting the situation you're in, learning to see and appreciate the positives, or solving a problem yourself. If you're chronically discontent, you're that much more likely to be overwhelmed when you encounter new stress.

When you find yourself wishing that things were different, challenge yourself. Ask yourself whether the situation is one you truly want or need to address. Perhaps you have a habit of responding to even minor annoyances by wishing things were different. If it doesn't really matter or is out of your control, then find a different way of commenting on it. Maybe you could practice mindfulness by saying, "That is this moment. Only this moment." You could also say, "Letting go, letting go," as a way of acknowledging and releasing unnecessary upset and judgment. "It is what it is" could help with acceptance.

Complaining

Mindfulness, again, means seeing and accepting reality as it is without judgment. When you complain, you're not accepting reality as it is. Complaining is a way of saying that situations, people, and life should be different than they are. Complaining is different than problem-solving.

When you complain, you're focused on what's wrong rather than what's right with the world. Over time, if you complain a lot, you may find that you're focused more on what you don't like than what you like about your day. You may even ignore the positives and only focus on what didn't go well. In that way, your reality can become distorted and your suffering may increase.

Using "Should"

Another way of not accepting reality is to say that people shouldn't do certain things. For example, you might believe that your daughter shouldn't have quit her job to tour with a band. Your daughter is taking a high risk by quitting her job, one that's unlikely to pay off and will probably have negative consequences. In that case, perhaps you're using "should" to point to a better or safer choice.

You might also use "should" to indicate that something doesn't fit your sense of fairness—for example, children "shouldn't" get cancer, or you "shouldn't" have lost those valuable, irreplaceable photographs of your family.

When you say that things that can and do happen shouldn't happen, you're not accepting reality as it is. Lack of acceptance brings suffering. Maybe, instead of using "should," you could say you're worried about the consequences of a certain action or that you're sad and hurt by an event.

Avoiding

Avoiding difficult situations typically leads to increased anxiety and having to endure even more difficult situations later. For example, not going to the doctor for fear something is wrong with you could have serious consequences. Avoiding someone who's upset with you may lead to loss of the relationship. There are many ways of avoiding, and most if not all are ways of not accepting reality. If you're mindful, you'll notice your fear and not let it control you.

Awareness of Nonacceptance

For a day, or even just an hour, notice when you're complaining, using "should," avoiding, or wishing things were different. Just notice, and then bring yourself back to the present moment and reality. Say something that promotes acceptance, such as "I accept what I cannot change." Remember, acceptance isn't about agreeing with the way things are—it's simply an acknowledgment that reality is what it is (Brach 2004).

Putting It All Together

Learning to be mindful of your emotions (and the events that triggered them is a critical skill in emotion management). Staying in the moment, not judging, and accepting your emotions are all part of mindfulness practice. The next step is to accurately label what you feel, which is covered in the next chapter.

CHAPTER 5

Identifying Your Emotions

Although you were born with the ability to experience basic emotions, you didn't enter this world knowing the names of those emotions. You learned to label your emotions in much the same way that you acquired the meanings of other words. For example, if you made a face and screamed, your parent said to you: "Oh, are you angry? You lost your toy? I see—you're sad because you miss your toy. Where is it? Let's look for it." In those few sentences, your parent guessed your emotion, identified the cause for the emotion, corrected the guess, and modeled problem solving. This is one way children learn basic emotion management.

If parents or other caretakers are emotionally skillful, the process of teaching children to recognize body sensations and label them accurately works smoothly. However, many caregivers are emotionally sensitive themselves or have difficulty managing their feelings. As a result, perhaps no one in your early life was able to teach you or model how to manage emotions effectively or even how to recognize emotions at all. Perhaps you were taught to avoid, hide, or fear your feelings.

How Identifying Your Emotions Helps

There's a physiological reason that knowing what you're feeling is so helpful in managing your emotions. The *amygdala* is the part of the brain that initiates the fight-or-flight reaction to help you deal with emergencies. It acts without much thought. When you name your feeling, that helps the *prefrontal cortex*, the executive center of the brain that's in charge of analytic and rational thought, stay in charge. When you label an emotion, you activate the brain's brake pedal (Lieberman 2006). The prefrontal cortex tells the amygdala to calm down. This helps you not act impulsively.

In addition to helping you not act impulsively, accurately naming what you're feeling gives you information (Linehan 1993). Anger, for example, usually means there's a problem to solve. If you don't recognize anger—or you mislabel it as, say, depression—you may not consider that there's a situation that you need to change in some way. The problem would stay the same, and your misery would increase. If you don't recognize shame, you may think you don't like to be around people, when actually you're afraid of being excluded. You'd then withdraw more, which would make the situation worse.

Knowing what you're feeling will help you connect to the cause of the feeling. If you're sad, for example, you can think back to what might have made you feel sad. Knowing the cause means you can think about what actions you can take to solve the problem, get more information, or accept the situation as one you cannot change. For example, maybe you realize you're sad because your friend didn't come to your birthday party. You can then let your friend know that you missed him. If you mislabel your sadness as anger, then your actions would likely be much different. You might stop talking with your friend or lose your temper with him. That wouldn't help with your sadness and could lead to losing the friendship, which may have been your original fear.

Strategies for Identifying Your Emotions

While everyone must cope with difficult feelings, emotionally sensitive people require the most effective emotion management skills they can develop. These skills include recognizing body sensations and labeling your emotions accurately. Learning to identify your emotions accurately will be a big step to feeling in control again.

Analyze Your Physical Sensations

If you aren't sure what emotion you're experiencing, pay attention to your physical experience. Emotions are felt as sensations in the body (Linehan 1993). Fear is often felt in the belly; anger, in the shoulders, back, and face; and sadness, in the chest and maybe the throat. Learn to recognize the sensations that signal certain emotions. For example, maybe you become tired whenever you're angry or have a headache when you're anxious. Maybe you have an upset stomach when you have to do something you dread.

If you tend not to recognize when you're experiencing an emotion, being attuned to your physical sensations can help you be more aware of your emotions. Whenever you have a physical sensation in response to an external event (for example, something that someone says or does) or that arises mysteriously, you can know to look for the emotion you would expect to result from that event and ask yourself whether that's what you're feeling.

What's Your Body Telling You?

Even if you often have trouble identifying your emotions, sometimes it's pretty clear what you're feeling. For example, when you're watching a sad movie, you probably feel sad. Practice recognizing the body sensations that go along with your emotions at those times. Over the next week, whenever you feel sad, angry, hurt, jealous, joyful, lonely, guilty, excited, happy, or ashamed, notice the body sensations that you have. Write them down on the chart that follows (or make your own chart). Also notice body sensations, including headaches, stomach upset, stomachaches, and fatigue, that you experience in response to things that happen or things that people say. Record that information on the chart as well, then guess as to the emotion.

Emotion	Body Sensations

After completing this exercise, you'll likely have a good idea about where in your body you experience emotions and can use that as a guide when you're unsure what you're feeling. Of course, headaches and other pain may be physical in origin, but even physical pain can be aggravated or exacerbated by emotions. If you have a headache and you know you usually get headaches when you're anxious, then you can look for what might be making you anxious. If you usually feel sadness behind your eyes or in your throat and that's where you're experiencing sensations, then you could look for what might have triggered sadness.

Analyze Your Urges to Act on Your Emotion

Emotions usually have actions associated with them. When you're experiencing an emotion, the action you want to take can offer a clue to what you might be feeling. For example, the urge to run away may indicate fear. The urge to hide and avoid eye contact may indicate shame. The urge to attack often indicates anger (Linehan 1993).

If you're emotionally sensitive, you may act according to your mood more often than others do. You may be active with friends and interested in the events of the day when you're happy or content but withdraw when you're depressed or sad. In addition, the way you see yourself may be controlled by your mood. You may hate yourself when you're angry or hurt, but you may like yourself, or at least not feel such intense self-dislike, when you're happy.

Though you probably have a strong inclination to act on your emotion, actually doing so is a choice. Remember from chapter 2 that if you act in ways that are consistent with an emotion, you're likely to increase the intensity of that emotion. Think about the feeling that's making you want to act in a certain way: Do you want to increase that feeling? If not, then change the action. Instead of hiding when you feel ashamed, hold your head high and be social. Instead of withdrawing when you feel depressed, push yourself to be more active and involved. In most situations, doing so will help you change the emotions you're feeling or at least not increase their intensity (Linehan 1993).

Determine the Cause of Your Emotion

Knowing the cause of your emotion is another way to identify what you're feeling (Linehan 1993). When you're searching for the cause of your emotional experience, look at events that happened recently, thoughts that you're having, and what you may have felt at first (i.e., primary emotions) that led you to feel the way you do now. You may find it helpful to start with a focus on events. Although thoughts can certainly cause emotions (as discussed below), often those thoughts were triggered by external events.

For example, imagine that you're enjoying breakfast when suddenly you have an uncomfortable feeling. Then you notice that you're thinking about your ex and identify the feeling as sadness. You may believe that thoughts of your ex brought on the sadness. However, the fact that you were enjoying a dish that your ex particularly liked led to thoughts about your ex. Then the sadness followed the thoughts. Thus the ultimate cause of your sadness was what you were eating for breakfast.

Think back to what you were doing or thinking or what was happening when you first felt the emotion. At first, you may not remember the details and believe that nothing particular happened that might create an emotional response. If so, go through your day, step by step, from the moment you got out of bed. For example, were you feeling this emotion when you woke up? At breakfast? When you went to work? During your lunch break? Look at what you did, what you heard, and what you thought since the last time you know you weren't feeling the emotion. Think about whom you talked with and what you talked about. If you still can't connect your emotion to any event, try to identify anything that happened in your day that would likely create an emotion in someone else. For example, most people would feel disappointed if a friend told them she couldn't make it for a planned movie night, as your friend told you today. Maybe that's the emotion you're having and couldn't identify.

A Few More Options

Another strategy for identifying what emotion you're feeling is to look carefully at a list of emotions. You may more easily recognize your emotion when given choices. Start with the basics, such as joy, surprise, anger/frustration, shame, guilt, fear, anxiety, and envy. Go through the various choices until you find a label that seems to fit your experience.

Paying attention to your body language, especially your facial expression, may work too. You may want to look in the mirror to see what your expression communicates. If your face looks sad, maybe that's what you're feeling. If you have difficulty identifying the emotion conveyed by your expression, maybe have others tell you what they see. Then you can check for any possible causes of that emotion, both to confirm and to know what action is most appropriate in the situation.

You may also pay attention to the thoughts you're having. If your thoughts are sad, you're likely to be experiencing sadness. The same goes for other types of thoughts. The way you think about a certain situation can trigger emotions, so being careful about your thinking will help you manage your emotions. You'll learn more about this in the next chapter.

Difficulties in Identifying Your Emotions

Knowing what you're feeling isn't easy, for many reasons. Maybe you don't notice the physical sensations that go with your emotions. Perhaps you incorrectly learned early in life to label all physical sensations as anger. Maybe you never learned the names of your emotions at all, or you push emotions away for as long as you can, saying you don't feel anything. Maybe you are confused about your emotions.

Emotion Confusion

Some body sensations and emotions are easily confused, such as fatigue and depression or excitement and happiness. In addition, emotional reactions can be complex and sometimes involve multiple feelings and thoughts. In some situations, you may mislabel thoughts as feelings. All of these possibilities can make it difficult to know what you're feeling.

Even when you're generally aware of what you're feeling, you may confuse one emotion for another, just like Ellen did in the following story.

> When Ellen was in her thirties, Christmas at her house was a huge production. She hand-dipped her own chocolates, decorated two trees, painted her Christmas cards, and cooked an elaborate meal for Christmas Eve. The process took months. Preparation for Christmas became so demanding that finally she couldn't budget the time any longer. She decided it had to stop. The following Christmas, she didn't put up a tree and she didn't cook. She was sad and at the same time relieved, because she just didn't have time to do the work.
>
> Ellen expected to not enjoy the holiday without all her usual preparations, but she did. She had a lovely, low-key holiday. She realized that she routinely confused happiness and excitement. Her elaborate preparations created excitement, not happiness. Accurately labeling her emotion changed the way she celebrated Christmas from then on.

Other emotions that can also be easily confused are excitement and anxiety. With anxiety, there's a sense of dread, while excitement entails more of a sense of expectation. A trip abroad may lead to both anxiety and excitement. So could a new, challenging job. When you mislabel excitement as anxiety, you may decide to avoid opportunities that you'd actually enjoy. At best, you'll experience unnecessary discomfort.

Anxiety and fear are sometimes mislabeled as well. Anxiety is often more about unpleasant events that might happen in the future, usually events over which you have no control. For example, you might feel anxious about whether you'll be hired for a job you want. Fear is about imminent danger, such as that someone might be breaking into your house right now.

Fear is useful when it helps you take action that you need to take, such as calling 911 or running from gunfire; or something less urgent but still important, such as getting to work on time when the boss is firing people who are late. Fear based on facts is helpful for problem solving and safety. Anxiety is helpful if it motivates you to solve a problem or prepare for a future event, such as practicing for a speech or studying for a test, but not so helpful when it's about situations for which no action is possible at the moment or over which you have no control.

Accurately labeling your feelings will help you know what actions to take to cope with the situation. If you're anxious about keeping your job, then using that anxiety to push yourself to be an even more valued employee or to look for another job could be helpful. On the other hand, if you're already doing all you can or if the situation is out of your control, then you could use specific techniques for managing the symptoms of anxiety, such as distraction or relaxing your muscles (see chapter 2).

Complex Emotional Experiences

As discussed above, people typically experience multiple feelings at the same time, but sometimes they're aware of or focus on only one.

For example, emotionally sensitive people often say they know they have a good life, yet they dwell on the one aspect that isn't going right. Being aware of only the one emotion limits your view of your life. When you feel sad, you may not notice any happiness that's also present. Maybe you're mostly sad, but at the same time you also feel joy or gratitude for your family, your home, and your friends.

When you feel multiple emotions at the same time about the same event, it can be difficult to label your emotions accurately. Let's say you're leaving the people you've worked with for years to move to a different city. You're sad about leaving your friends but also happy, excited, and anxious about the new opportunity. Maybe you have regrets or guilt about past issues with your coworkers. It can be hard to pick all these emotions apart.

Noticing emotions other than the one that dominates may mean searching for what else you're feeling. Doing so will help you stay balanced. You'll have a better sense of your overall emotional experience and be less overwhelmed by difficult emotions.

Completing the following exercise will increase your awareness of your feelings and give you practice labeling your emotions.

Your Emotional Life

For one week, pay careful attention to accurately labeling your emotions. In the following spaces, on a separate piece of paper, or on the worksheet available at http://www.newharbinger.com/29934, record the emotions you feel each day. Some common emotions are listed below.

Sadness	Anger	Anxiety
Fear	Jealousy	Love
Hurt	Frustration	Joy

Day 1: ____

Day 2: ____

Day 3: ____

Day 4: ____

Day 5: ____

Day 6: ____

Day 7: ____

At the end of the week, review what you wrote. If you felt any particular emotion most of the time, or you noticed only one or two emotions each day, then try again for another week, looking even more carefully for more emotions. For example, if you're anxious most of the time, notice other emotions that you have, such as moments of joy or flashes of anger. Check in with yourself frequently to see what you might be feeling. You may find it helpful to create a reminder to periodically be aware of what you're feeling—for instance, by setting your watch to beep every hour.

Combined Thoughts and Emotions

Emotions can combine with thoughts to create other emotions. For example, disappointment is usually the result of thoughts that your expectations weren't met and feelings of sadness. Frustration is a combination of believing you can solve a problem and anger over the difficulty of actually doing so (Conley 2012). In other words, what you think can affect your feelings. This can make it hard to identify the initial emotion.

Emotions Can Trigger Other Thoughts and Emotions

Sometimes having an emotion in relation to an event or a thought about an event triggers other emotions. Perhaps you're afraid of feeling sad. So when you feel sad, you become scared. Or maybe you don't like feeling sad, so you become angry as a way of avoiding sadness.

Let's say you're sad because your wife lost her job. You become angry to replace the sadness, because you hate feeling sad—you feel less vulnerable when you're angry. When you see your wife, you speak to her coldly. Maybe you accuse her of being lazy. Then she argues back and says hurtful things to you. Your actions made the problem worse. Now you feel miserable.

Identifying your initial emotion is important to coping effectively, because that's the emotion that's directly connected to your experience.

Thoughts vs. Feelings

When you did the exercise "Your Emotional Life," you may have been unsure at times what was a thought and what was a feeling. Emotionally sensitive people often confuse the two. For example, you may often say "I feel" rather than "I think." As a result, you may bring feelings into a situation where they're not applicable or helpful. Let's say you're selecting a leader for a workgroup. Saying "*I feel* George would be a good leader" makes the statement emotional, even if you evaluated George's leadership abilities in a logical way. It also makes you more likely to react emotionally if anyone disagrees with you. Saying "*I think* George would be a good leader" takes the statement out of the emotional realm. Expressing thoughts clearly as thoughts, not feelings, will help you separate your emotional reactions from your logical thinking.

Some unpleasant thoughts are particularly easy to confuse with feelings, and the confusion makes coping with them more difficult. Imagine that your friend reveals to others information you shared with her privately. You might say "I feel so betrayed." And you probably have no idea how to cope with feeling betrayed. That's because "betrayed" isn't a feeling; it's a thought. To be more accurate, you'd say "I was betrayed," or "I know she betrayed me." Recognizing in this way that "betrayed" is a thought will lead you to appropriate action. You might decide to check out the truth of the situation or to be more cautious in your interactions with this particular friend; or you might decide to not be friends.

Your *feelings about the betrayal* are different than your thoughts, and not about logic. When someone betrays you, you may feel sad, angry, and/or hurt. Identifying how you feel will allow you to choose ways to cope effectively with those emotions. If you're sad, you might choose to comfort yourself. If you're angry, you might give yourself some time to cool off before making any decisions.

Both your thoughts and your feelings about being betrayed are part of the experience of being betrayed, and recognizing the combination will give you a more accurate understanding of it. Perhaps saying "I feel betrayed" is a shorthand way of relating that total experience, but it doesn't fully or accurately express your thoughts and feelings, and that makes coping with the situation harder.

What if you were to say "I feel broken"? Like "betrayed," "broken" isn't a feeling. Expressing the thought *I'm broken* as a feeling actually masks what you're really feeling. To reword the statement to reflect both your feelings and your thoughts, you might say "I think I'm broken because I see myself as abandoned by others" or "I feel a painful sadness that rips me apart inside."

Identifying your experience specifically and accurately will help you act with wisdom. You will also be less likely to base your view of yourself on what may be inaccurate thoughts labeled as feelings.

Thought or Feeling?

In this exercise, you'll practice distinguishing between thoughts and feelings. Place a check mark next to those sentences that are accurately worded as feelings. Place an X next to those sentences that could be more accurately worded. Think of a situation—perhaps one you've actually experienced—that might fit the sentiment, and then imagine how you might reword the sentence. (Do this exercise now for optimal understanding and benefit from the rest of the chapter.)

____ 1. *I feel left out.*

____ 2. *I feel like a failure.*

____ 3. *I'm pretty.*

____ 4. *I must have chocolate right now.*

____ 5. *I feel so jealous I could rip her head off.*

____ 6. *I feel confused.*

____ 7. *I feel hurt.*

____ 8. *I feel disconnected.*

____ 9. *I love potato chips.*

____ 10. *I feel so clumsy.*

Answers

Statements 5 and 7 are feelings. The rest are thoughts. Go back and look at the ones you missed. For example, the statement "I feel like a failure" is a thought mislabeled as a feeling. The feelings that go with thinking you're a failure might be sadness, despair, embarrassment, or shame. See whether you can change the sentence to state the thought and the feeling(s) separately—for example, "I think I fail at most things I do, and I feel embarrassed and sad that I was fired from my job." If this was a real example from your life, it would be helpful to state things in this way rather than "I feel like a failure," because you could then check the facts to see whether it was true that you fail at most things you do, as well as address the embarrassment and sadness you just accurately expressed.

The Problem of Numbed Emotions

It's difficult to identify what you're feeling if you're using food, other substances (like pain pills), or activities (like self-harm, overworking, excessive shopping, obsessing, or excessive exercise) to numb your feelings. Try to be aware of your urges to overeat or to busy yourself with some other activity when you feel something negative, and first consider what emotion you might be having. Practice letting yourself experience that emotion.

Awareness of How You Numb Your Emotions

Choose one behavior that you know you use to numb unwanted emotions. Some possibilities are shopping, eating, drinking alcohol, working, using the computer or phone, excessive busyness, sleeping, socializing, and hibernating. Whatever it is, write the behavior you use to numb yourself in the space below (or download this worksheet from http://www.newharbinger.com/29934).

For the next week, each time you want to numb yourself, set a timer for three minutes. Take that time to think about and then write down the feelings and thoughts that are behind your urge. Take the full three minutes, if you can, to help you realize emotions that may not be obvious. The emotions and thoughts behind your urge to numb may be different at different times, or you may find you have a consistent pattern.

Numbing activity: ______________________________

Feelings: ______________________________

Thoughts: ______________________________

Feelings: ____

Thoughts: ____

Feelings: ____

Thoughts: ____

Feelings: ____

Thoughts: ____

Feelings: ____

Thoughts: ____

Feelings: ____

Thoughts: ____

Feelings: ____

Thoughts: ____

In doing the exercise above, maybe you found that the emotion you wanted to numb was always the same, like sadness; or maybe you found that you wanted to numb all emotions. As you go forward, pay particular attention to those emotions you tend to avoid. Practice not numbing those emotions by just feeling them for a period of time. Allow yourself to feel the emotion until it dissipates. If that's too intense, then set a time frame that you can manage, such as five minutes, during which you'll experience the emotion before distracting yourself in a healthy way, such as through physical exercise or talking with a friend. You'll find the emotion will pass. Note that when you're aware of an emotion and allow yourself to experience it, you can take planned breaks from it through activities. In this way you're not avoiding the emotion.

Making False Assumptions or Incorrectly Identifying the Cause of Your Emotion

When people don't know the reasons why they feel what they feel, they may arrive at conclusions that seem quite logical but aren't correct. If you're emotionally sensitive, you may be unaware that you can be quite adept at formulating explanations for your emotions that aren't necessarily true.

Sometimes you may invent reasons for the way you're feeling because, as discussed, the true causes can be complex, making them difficult to identify. For example, in certain situations you may be aware only of secondary emotions (i.e., the emotions you have in reaction to other emotions). Perhaps you experience anger whenever you feel sad, and the anger is so automatic that you're not aware of the sadness that came first.

Emotionally sensitive people are typically creative. Creative thinking can mean that you make connections between events that others don't (Ariely 2012). Most of the time, your ability to see and comprehend the world in a different way is an advantage (e.g., Pink 2005). However, sometimes you may view events as related when they're not. You may exaggerate your mistakes or attribute responsibility to yourself for events that weren't your fault. You may convince yourself you're responsible for other people's moods and actions. It can be helpful to know if you have a knack for seeing events in a self-blaming way.

Interpreting events as your fault when they're not adds unnecessary pain to your life. To change this pattern, try not to read any hidden meaning into others' behaviors or words. If you have thoughts about their behavior or words, look at the facts of the situation and get all the information before accepting responsibility.

Being clear about the difference between facts and interpretations is important in managing emotions (Linehan 1993). Facts are events that you can observe directly. You can observe someone frown, but you can only guess the reason for the frown. Only the person frowning can know the reason. When you think something might be true, be sure to ask rather than make assumptions, no matter how right you think your guesses are.

Making assumptions about others' thoughts and the reasons for their behavior often creates painful moments. Consider how your thinking might be strengthening your negative emotions. Focusing on ideas such as *She's trying to get me fired* will increase your anxiety. Thoughts such as *He hasn't returned my call—he must want to break up with me* may increase your anger, anxiety, and sadness. Just because you have a thought doesn't mean the thought is true. Try to find the truth, so that you don't create or build overwhelming feelings based on misinterpretations or false assumptions.

For example, imagine that you feel anxious but aren't sure why. You think about it and then realize that a good friend hasn't contacted you in a while. You think of times when you might have upset her. You attempt to talk with your friend about why she's upset with you. When she says there's no problem, you don't believe her. You decide there's no way to save the relationship because she won't talk with you about the problem. So, hurt and fearful of rejection, you avoid her.

Though you're intuitive, it could be that your friend isn't upset with you. Perhaps she's just busy or worried about something else in her life. You may be right about her upset feelings but not about the reason for them. Or it could be that your anxiety isn't about your friend at all. Perhaps you're uncomfortable because your daughter is moving to another state and you worry about her being far away. You don't want to think about her moving, because that's too scary. It's less painful to interpret your anxiety as having to do with your friend being angry with you.

If you have a history of making false assumptions or of incorrectly identifying reasons for your feelings, as illustrated above, you may have stopped trusting yourself to know why you feel the way you do. If so, then carefully reviewing the events that preceded your emotion and not making assumptions will be important to regaining trust in your ability to know your own emotions.

The following worksheet can help you look more closely at how your emotions affect you.

Your Emotional Habits

Over the next week, whenever you have an emotional reaction to an event, fill out the My Emotions and Behavior worksheet. (You can download a full-size version from http://www.newharbinger.com/29934.)

First, describe the event. For example, maybe your best friend didn't call to wish you well on your job interview.

Next, record any thoughts you might have had—thoughts like *She doesn't care about me*, or *She's always been selfish; I don't know why I expected anything different.*

Next, record the first emotion you experienced (anger, sadness, fear, jealousy, joy, love) and then record any emotions resulting from your initial emotion. Maybe you feel anger whenever you feel sadness.

Next, list what information your emotion is giving you. For example, hurt might tell you that you value your best friend's support. Anger might tell you to problem solve with your friend or stand up for yourself.

Next, write what you actually did after having the emotion. Did you overeat? Avoid your friend? Withdraw?

Finally, write the results of your actions, both positive and negative, short-term and long-term. Did you find a beautiful new jacket and spend too much money on items you didn't need? Did you have a fight with your friend that you later regretted?

My Emotions and Behavior

Event: ____

Trigger thoughts: ______________________________________

First emotion: ______________ Second emotion: ______________

Info: ____

Action: ____

Results (short-term and long-term): ______________________

____

Event: ____

Trigger thoughts: ______________________________________

First emotion: ______________ Second emotion: ______________

Info: ____

Action: ____

Results (short-term and long-term): ______________________

____

Event: ____

Trigger thoughts: ______________________________________

First emotion: ______________ Second emotion: ______________

Info: ____

Action: ____

Results (short-term and long-term): ______________________

____

Event: ____

Trigger thoughts: ________________________________

First emotion: ______________ Second emotion: ______________

Info: ____

Action: ____

Results (short-term and long-term): __________________________

____

Event: ____

Trigger thoughts: ________________________________

First emotion: ______________ Second emotion: ______________

Info: ____

Action: ____

Results (short-term and long-term): __________________________

____

When you have a week's worth of information, look over what you wrote. Check for emotional patterns. Perhaps you typically go shopping when you feel sad, or you blame yourself when someone's upset. Maybe when you think mean thoughts about yourself, you tend to feel angry or sad. If this is the case, figure out ways to change the pattern. Perhaps what brings about your emotions is something that you can change. Maybe waking up to dirty dishes brings the thought that you're a lazy slob, which triggers hopelessness, and that leads to not wanting to leave the house or be active in any way. The long-term consequences are that you don't make progress toward goals that are important to you, such as taking classes or making more friends. Not having dirty dishes waiting for you in the morning could change your mood.

Putting It All Together

Accurately identifying your emotions is critical for emotion management. That goes for anyone. If you're emotionally sensitive, it's even more important to know and strengthen the ways you can manage your feelings, because your emotions can be so intense. Once you're skilled at using the strategies you've learned in this chapter to identify your emotions and their causes, understanding how you respond to specific emotions will help you cope with them more effectively. In later chapters, you'll learn other ways of changing your emotional patterns. For example, in the next chapter, you'll learn about letting go of judgments about yourself, others, and the world, which tend to add to your emotions and make you more likely to be overwhelmed by your emotional experiences.

CHAPTER 6

Letting Go of Judgments

If you're emotionally sensitive, it may be that ever since you were a child, people have said or implied there's something wrong with the way you feel and think. Comments such as these, as well as the mere thought that people are judging you in this way, have probably been such a source of pain for so many years that you're hypersensitive to any hint of criticism. Although no one likes to be judged negatively, for the emotionally sensitive it's agonizing. Negative judgments, both actual and imagined, may often lead you to feel shame and to experience hopeless thoughts, as well as to fear rejection.

Even positive judgments, such as saying something is "good," can be problematic, because if one thing is "good," then a different thing might be "bad." In this way, positive judgments maintain your potential for negative judgments. They strengthen your tendency to make comparisons and see things in terms of their "good" and "bad" qualities. Although, for the most part, you may assume that when I talk about judging in this chapter, I mean making negative judgments, keep in mind that making positive judgments can also contribute to the issue in almost every case.

Letting go of self-judgments, others' judgments of you, and your judgments of others, whether positive or negative, is one way of keeping your emotions at a lower intensity (Linehan 1993). The point isn't to have a more positive view of everything but to stop thinking so much in terms of good versus bad (or any other duality) and just accept that things are what they are. When you replace judgments with facts, you'll react less to misinterpretations, assumptions, and distortions about events and people.

Self-Judgment

Judging creates emotion. In addition, any emotion you feel in response to an external event will be intensified if you judge yourself for that event. For example, if you're getting divorced and you judge yourself as unlovable or as someone who always messes up, the intense pain of divorce will become worse. If you then judge yourself for being upset, that will add more pain. Increasing your awareness of your self-judgments and better understanding the way you learned to judge yourself in a particular way can help you reduce this behavior.

If you were an emotionally sensitive child, maybe you were told you were too dramatic, emotional, needy, weak, manipulative, or attention-seeking. You might have been told to stop "being a baby" or "making a big deal out of nothing." Maybe you were ignored or were considered a burden. Being judged by others when you were a child can lead you to judge yourself in the same way as an adult.

You may blame yourself for all sorts of flaws. For example, you might believe that if you weren't so lazy you'd have gotten a job by now, even though you've put in five applications a day for the past two weeks. But even if you haven't submitted any applications, that doesn't automatically mean you're lazy. If you look more closely at the facts, you may realize that your fear of being judged negatively, not laziness, has kept you from applying for jobs.

Self-judgment and fear of being judged will keep you trapped. Instead of living your life the way you want, you'll try to live safely, doing what others deem acceptable. You may try to fit into molds that aren't right for you. There's no winning in this scenario.

The following exercise can help you identify how people in your life have judged you and help you get at the truth about yourself.

Judgments by Others

How did important people in your life habitually describe you when you were a child? Were you "cute," "smart," "lazy," "athletic," or "a baby"? On the following chart (which you can download in full-scale form from http://www.newharbinger.com/29934), list as many descriptors as you can. Then go back and look for evidence of each one. Write down what exactly you did that led people to describe you that way. For example, if people called you "a baby," maybe you cried before school every day. Now consider and write down the reasons for those behaviors. In the example of crying before school, maybe you were scared of performing poorly in school or getting into trouble.

Descriptor	What Behaviors Fit the Descriptor?	Actual Reasons for Behavior

Now think about what you've written. All of us have flaws. You may find that some of the ways people described you were accurate. At the same time, pay close attention to the situations you were in and how much of an impact your circumstances had on your behavior at the time. Your behavior is strongly influenced by what's happening in your life at the moment. Chances are very good that you had sensible reasons for behaving the way you did, and those reasons probably had to do with the situation, not your character.

The Problems with Judgments

Judgments can make managing your emotions more difficult in other ways as well. Judging interferes with decision making, identifying emotions accurately, and preserving relationships. Judgments can also limit your view of the world. Let's look at these problems more closely.

Judgments Interfere with Decision-Making and Problem-Solving Skills

When you're emotional, the analytic part of your brain isn't fully engaged. You behave in ways that reflect your emotion, not the truth of the situation. This is true for everyone. If you're emotionally sensitive, however, it happens more frequently. Judgments can quickly increase your emotional distress and cloud your thinking.

For example, imagine that you text your friend to invite him to lunch tomorrow. You keep checking your phone, because he usually texts you back right away. After ten minutes, you're aggravated. *Why isn't he answering?* You may judge yourself at this point, saying you were stupid to ask him to lunch. After more time passes, you may go over the last time you talked, judging yourself as having been too selfish and saying all the wrong things. As time goes on, you may judge your friend as inconsiderate and a user who just pretended to like you. This may continue until you become emotionally overwhelmed with hurt, anger, and fear. You may decide that you'll never speak to your friend again. When he calls later in the day, you don't answer.

Your judgments of your friend and yourself created emotional distress and interfered with your thinking. Remember that you couldn't have known the reason he didn't answer your message right away. Maybe his phone wasn't charged, maybe he was in a long meeting, or maybe he didn't receive the text.

Judgments Hide Primary Feelings

Judging other people interferes with managing your emotions because it masks your primary emotions. For example, imagine that you go to a restaurant and see your boyfriend having lunch with an attractive woman. You're furious. *That jerk is nothing but a player*, you think. You tell him off and storm out of there. Anger was probably your secondary emotion, however. Most likely, the first emotion you felt was fear: fear of being hurt, fear of losing someone you love, and fear of being rejected. When you said to yourself, *That jerk is nothing but a player*, that hid your fear, your primary emotion. Any time you focus on a secondary emotion, you'll likely have limited success in coping with the situation, because the first emotion you experienced is the one you need to address. If you had said to yourself: *My boyfriend is having lunch with an attractive woman. I'm terrified that he's cheating and I'll be hurt*, then you would've been recognizing and labeling your emotions and saying what you knew to be true, with no assumptions. You would've had more success at staying in emotional control because you could've used skills for coping with fear, the primary emotion, such as finding out the truth of the situation before making assumptions (see chapter 2).

Judgments Add to Your Loneliness

Most emotionally sensitive people say they often feel lonely. Any time you judge your friends, your coworkers, your neighbors, and even strangers as different from you in some way, you're setting yourself apart from them rather than creating connections, which can add to the loneliness you feel.

Judging other people creates reasons to not be friendly. Maybe there's someone who's now a good friend of yours but whom you thought of in judgmental ways when you first met. That probably got in the way of your getting to know this person better.

Judging can put distance between you and those you love. People will always make mistakes. If you judge a loved one for making a mistake, you'll damage the relationship. For example, imagine your wife comes home with a speeding ticket. If you say that she's a no-brained excuse for a wife who just wasted your hard-earned money, you're not strengthening your relationship. If you say, "I'm worried about the cost of the ticket, and that scares me," you're expressing your feelings without judgment.

Judgments Narrow Your View

Judging events without having all the information or recognizing that the picture keeps changing creates emotional ups and downs. You judge one event as bad and react to that; you judge another event as good and react to that. If you stop judging, you'll stop that emotional roller coaster.

For example: When your sister tells a secret that you told her not to tell, you judge her as disloyal and a traitor. You decide you don't want her in your life anymore. Then the next day, you're sorry that you reacted that way. You recognize that although she slipped up and told your secret, she has also given you a place to live after your divorce and has sat with you for hours when you were upset. In the heat of the moment, you saw only the event that had just occurred, rather than the whole relationship.

Changing Judgmental Thinking

When we practice something or do it often, we get better at it. This applies to the way we think as much as to anything else. The more you think in a judgmental way, the more automatic that way of thinking will become. When you practice not being judgmental, you'll become less judgmental. This is one of the reasons that being nonjudgmental about everyday situations is important. Not being judgmental about the small issues is practice for the big issues.

Letting Go of Judgments

You'll always think judgmental thoughts, and some days you'll experience more of those thoughts than other days. The number of judgments that come into your mind isn't particularly important. The goal is to notice those thoughts and not get hooked into believing them or letting them influence your emotions.

You may judge automatically without noticing what you are doing. Becoming aware of how often you make judgments will help you to change your thinking.

Counting Your Judgments

Choose a day to count your judgments. For that day, count your judgmental statements and thoughts, both positive and negative. Include both judgments about yourself and judgments about others. Consider setting your watch to chime periodically as a reminder to notice your judging. Watch for words that represent absolutes or extremes, such as "always" and "never," and comparison words, such as "better" and "worse," because these often signal judgments. Name calling, such as "jerk" or "idiot," is judgmental.

If you count a large number, then letting go of judgments will be of great help in managing your emotions. If you don't judge very often, then letting go of judgments won't be as big a challenge.

Commit to Letting Go of Judgments

Any time you want to change your behavior, an important step is to make a commitment. So commit to letting go of judging. Decide that you want to let go of judging, and list the reasons why. Remember that practicing giving up even the judgments that seem to be harmless is important, because it'll help you be more successful when the situation is more challenging.

To help you make a commitment, write out your answers to the following questions.

1. How do your judgments of others affect your life? How do their judgments of you affect your life?
2. How are judgments useful to you? How are they harmful?
3. What are the reasons that you think it's important for you to stop judging (or not)?
4. How would your conversations be different if you didn't judge others?
5. How would your life be different if you didn't judge yourself?

Part of making a commitment is holding yourself accountable. Set a time period, such as six weeks, during which you'll practice letting go of your judgments, perhaps using one or more of the ideas in the sections that follow. (You can go ahead and finish the chapter before embarking on this exercise.) Consider marking the time period on a calendar and checking off each day. Create a reminder, such as a symbol of your commitment you can wear or carry (like a bracelet or a ring), or put sticky notes around your home and office to remind yourself to let go of judging. To help you stay on track, you can journal about your experiences each day, or team up with a partner and discuss your experiences daily or every other day.

At the end of the six weeks, write what changes you've noticed starting to happen in your ability to manage your emotions. Recording changes is important to help you see your progress.

Label the Judgment and Let It Pass

Once you've become more aware of your judgments, the next step is to label them as judgments and let them pass. When you notice you've judged a situation or person, say to yourself, *That's a judgment,* and go on with what you're doing. You may have to repeat the process several times. Simply practicing letting judgments pass without acting on them or believing them will lessen the power they have over your mood and behavior. With time, you'll be adept at saying, "That's a judgment," and going on with your day.

LET GO OF COMPARISONS BETWEEN YOU AND OTHER PEOPLE

If you're emotionally sensitive, you may be hyperalert as to how you fit or don't fit with various groups and other people in general. You may not realize you're typically choosing to compare yourself to others only in ways you see them as superior, which naturally makes you feel inferior in comparison. For example, you might compare yourself to a model for how you look in a swimsuit, a CEO for career achievement, and Martha Stewart for housekeeping. Or you may not realize that if you compare yourself favorably with someone, you're judging *that* person in a negative way.

REWORDING JUDGMENTS

You can reword your thoughts or statements so that you aren't using judgmental language. The statement "Chocolate ice cream is better than vanilla" is a judgment. On the other hand, "I prefer chocolate ice cream to vanilla" is a clear statement of preference.

You can practice letting go of judgments by changing a judgment into a goal for yourself or an appreciation of others' success. Instead of saying, "She always looks so put together, and I'm such a slob," perhaps you can say: "She's great at putting outfits together. I want to learn to do that." Instead of saying, "She thinks she's better than everyone else," maybe say: "She keeps getting promoted. I want that for myself."

Letting Go of Judgmental Language

Reword the statements that follow, taking out the judgment.

1. Why didn't *I* get that promotion? I'm smarter than anyone else at my work.
2. Cassey always gets the cute guys. I'm such a loser.
3. Everyone thinks Dave is so great. What's he got that makes him so special?
4. I'm unlovable. No one will ever care about me.

Remember that practicing letting go of judgments when the judgment seems harmless is important, because you're learning a way of thinking. Practice restating the following judgments as preferences.

1. That's a horrible shade of red.
2. My phone is the best there is.
3. Everyone knows you're a jerk, and I wouldn't go to the movies with you if you were the last person on Earth.
4. That car is the best car ever made.

CONSEQUENCES AND EMOTIONS

Judgments are often a way of saying that someone's actions may have a negative consequence. You can let go of judgments by stating the consequences explicitly. Stating the consequences instead of using "good" and "bad" will more fully communicate your meaning.

If you have a strong emotion about the consequences or behavior, be sure to include it in your statement (Linehan 1993). Instead of saying "That guy is bad," you might say "That guy was arrested for hitting his girlfriend, and I'm so scared she'll go back to him and get seriously hurt."

Expressing Emotional Intensity Without Judgments

Practice rewording the following statements to include the consequences and the emotions but leave out the judgments.

1. (You were charged a late fee on a bill.) I'm so stupid—I never pay attention—I can't believe I keep making the same stupid mistake over and over.

2. (Your boss corrected a typo on your report.) She's out to get me. She's so unfair—she hates me and she just wants to fire me.

3. (You didn't feel like keeping lunch plans you made with your friend. It has happened before, and your friend is angry.) What a loser I am. I screw everything up.

4. (You didn't understand the homework and got a bad grade.) You're a lousy teacher. I can't believe you have a job.

5. (You dented your friend's car.) I'm such a loser. I never do anything right.

6. (Your boss refuses to let you leave early on your last day before vacation.) He hates me and just wants to make my life miserable.

7. (Your significant other breaks up with you.) I'll be alone forever.

WITH WISDOM, ASSUME GOOD INTENTIONS

Emotionally sensitive people can be quite suspicious and see threats where no danger exists. This can create a whirlwind of emotional upset. For example, imagine that when you're at a party, one of your close friends (who's also at the party) barely talks with you. You decide that she hates you because of an upsetting event you shared with her the day before. You're sure she's telling everyone about the mistake you made. In reality, however, she's upset about her daughter breaking her engagement and is avoiding you because she isn't ready to discuss it with you. In such a situation, when you don't have evidence to support your negative judgments about what your friend is thinking, reword your thoughts to something like *I don't know what she's thinking.* Give your friend the benefit of the doubt by assuming she's being the best friend she can be, given her circumstances.

Assuming the Positive

If you assume others are against you, then you'll judge their actions differently than if you assume others have your best interests at heart.

For the next week, actively assume that the people you know have good intentions. Remind yourself to act in concordance with that idea, even when your loved ones act in ways you don't like. Put your relationship with them first, rather than letting daily annoyances or fears control your thoughts about them. You'll find that your relationships will be stronger and you'll be less upset.

PRACTICE COMPASSION FOR OTHERS (AND FOR YOURSELF)

If someone drops out of college several times, you might think he was irresponsible or spoiled. You'd be judging his character based on his having to stop going to school. A more compassionate response would be to feel regret for him that he had to drop out for whatever reason. Being more compassionate with others, as well as with yourself, can help you decrease your judgments.

Learning to give up judging others and yourself will be difficult. Practice being compassionate with yourself while you're working on making changes and doing the best that you can. Instead of saying you're hopeless, say, "Change takes time, and I need to be patient with myself in order to stay committed and reach my goal."

SELF-PUNISHMENT IS NOT A GOOD MOTIVATOR

You may believe if you didn't punish yourself you'd never get anything done or make any changes. You may think the only way you can accomplish goals is to beat yourself up emotionally. For example, if you don't call yourself a "fatty," you won't lose weight.

But negative judgments, particularly negative self-judgments, actually discourage you and make it difficult to achieve your goals. There's a reason cheerleaders at a football game shout "Go team!" Can you imagine them jeering "Forget it, you losers"? That wouldn't help the players work hard to succeed.

When you find yourself thinking punishing thoughts, notice the thoughts. Label them as "unhelpful thoughts" or just "thoughts." Search for self-compassionate words, and be understanding of yourself. Consider what you might say to a friend under the same circumstances. Being compassionate and accepting with yourself is much more likely to help you make the changes you'd like to make.

When Others Judge You

Because you cannot control other people's behavior, it's important to have skills to manage the thoughts and feelings that result from others' judgments about you. You'll likely need many skills to cope with the sadness, hurt, and shame that you feel. Practice using mindfulness to take a pause and not respond immediately to others' judgments. If needed, take a break. Use the skills in chapter 2 to help you calm your emotions. As always, if at all possible, don't respond until you can think with a clear mind (Linehan 1993).

You can also use the skills outlined in this chapter: Label the judgment and just let it pass rather than having it define who you are. Reword the judgment that was placed on you, leaving out the judgmental words. Look at just the facts. If you can learn from those facts, then focus on the lesson. Practice compassion for yourself and the other person.

Putting It All Together

Emotionally sensitive people are usually judgmental of themselves, the world, and others. Letting go of judgments is one of the most powerful steps you can take to be less overwhelmed by emotions on a daily basis. Practice replacing judgments with precise descriptions of situations and the consequences of those situations. Practice being compassionate and assuming good intentions on the part of others. While this may be a challenge, the results will be a calmer life, a more accurate view of yourself, and improved relationships.

CHAPTER 7

Learning Effective Decision Making

Emotionally sensitive people are often overwhelmed when faced with decisions. At the very time you need to be clear-headed, you may be flooded with emotion. Even everyday decisions, such as what to wear to a meeting or where to take your friends to dinner, can be a struggle.

Well-considered choices require that you consider the facts of the situation, know what you want, explore possible consequences, and be willing to compromise when necessary. Any time you're emotional, this process becomes more complicated and difficult.

Emotional Dilemmas

There are several ways emotions can derail your decision-making process. You may be too anxious or overwhelmed with other emotions to carefully analyze your options. You may be too afraid of failure or of other people's reactions to risk making a decision. Perhaps you're so focused on what you want in the moment that you cannot adequately consider the long-term consequences of any of the choices. You may not have a good sense of the difficulty of decision making and either underestimate or overestimate the amount of problem solving involved—when this is the case, you may become easily discouraged and give up before your solution has a chance to work.

Emotionally sensitive people tend to have certain emotional dilemmas that interfere with making decisions. The following questionnaire can help you identify the way you approach problems and make decisions. When you know your decision-making style, you can be more aware of the typical issues you're likely to face whenever you have to make a decision.

Your Emotional Dilemmas in Decision Making

Place a check mark in the space next to each of the following statements that are true for you at this point in time. If the statement isn't true about you most of the time, then leave the space blank.

____ 1. *I can go for days and not think about important decisions that I need to make. I keep myself busy doing other things, like reading, going to the gym, listening to music, and cleaning the house.*

____ 2. *When I need to make a decision, I almost always talk it over with others who make better choices than I do.*

____ 3. *I can't stand looking at the possible outcomes of different choices. I go with what I want, even though it usually doesn't work out well.*

____ 4. *When I try to make decisions, I become so overwhelmed with anxiety that I can't think. To get it over with, I just make a choice.*

____ 5. *I go over and over all the choices I could make and I get stuck. I keep thinking I'm missing something and will make the wrong choice.*

____ 6. *When faced with decisions, I get depressed. Often I just give up.*

____ 7. *I research every decision thoroughly. Sometimes I have so much information that I'm overwhelmed.*

____ 8. *I miss deadlines because I can't stop considering the costs and benefits of my decision.*

____ 9. *I put off decisions until sometimes there's no longer a decision to be made because I don't know what to do and I just don't have the energy to think about it.*

____ 10. *I don't make decisions because I just don't care.*

____ 11. *I often make important choices that I know are wrong for me because I listen to what other people want me to do.*

____ 12. *If other people decide on something, I'll usually go along.*

____ 13. *I make important choices based on what I want at the time and not on what I know is wisest.*

____ 14. *I'm not good at delaying decisions. I jump in and go full-speed ahead.*

____ 15. *I'm afraid of making decisions. So I just choose an option and hope for the best.*

____ 16. *When I need to make a decision, I avoid anything that would remind me about the decision.*

____ 17. *It's critical that I make the best choice every time, so I want every single piece of information I can have.*

____ 18. *I jump at what seem like good ideas, but often they don't work out.*

____ 19. *I'm not good at saying no to myself.*

____ 20. *If I want something now, I don't wait, even when it would be wiser to wait.*

____ 21. *I struggle to say no to others.*

____ 22. *I feel defeated about making decisions. Nothing ever works out anyway.*

____ 23. *I just let things happen.*

____ 24. *I ignore decisions and problems for as long as possible.*

____ 25. *I often feel paralyzed when faced with a decision or problem.*

Scoring: Indicate how many statements you checked from each of the following groups:

4, 14, 15, 18: ____ (Impulsive Approach)

5, 7, 8, 17: ____ (Overanalyzing Approach)

1, 16, 23, 24, 25: ____ (Passive Approach)

2, 11, 12, 21: ____ (Dependent Approach)

3, 13, 19, 20: ____ (Willful Approach)

6, 9, 10, 22: ____ (Defeatist Approach)

If you checked three or more statements from any one group, then the approach identified in parentheses is likely to be a part of your decision-making style. Each approach is described below.

The Impulsive Approach

Your anxiety about problem solving and decision making is so high that you aren't able to think clearly and you just want to get past the situation as quickly as possible. You don't think things through. You may say you don't care about the consequences. As a result, your choices often have undesired outcomes, which increase your self-doubt, and you become even more fearful of making decisions.

The Overanalyzing Approach

Although also the result of high anxiety and emotion about decision making, this is the opposite of the Impulsive Approach: you think without acting. You go through all the choices in detail and then repeatedly review them. You may know what choice you prefer but delay making that choice because you're afraid it's not the perfect one. You worry about endless "what ifs." You may focus on the downside of every option to the point you're paralyzed and the decision goes unmade until circumstances make the choice for you—for example, a college-enrollment deadline passes and you no longer have the option to take classes.

The Passive Approach

You attempt to not acknowledge problems at all. You ignore, don't think about, or put off considering issues, problems, or decisions that are scary. Sometimes you try to get someone else to make the decision just to get rid of your anxiety, but then you often don't want to act on those decisions either. Often you don't make a decision at all or you wait until you're forced to make one.

The Dependent Approach

You're overly focused on what other people think or would do. You seek their opinions, and when they explain what they'd do, their choices make sense to you, and that's what you decide is best. If you get different feedback from various people, you may vacillate, favoring whatever view you heard most recently. You may blame the person who gave you the advice if it doesn't work out. You also may make choices to avoid conflict rather than opting for what truly works.

The Willful Approach

You tend to make decisions based on what you want, not on facts or reasoning. You don't want to consider the pros and cons. You act as if you can make your desired choice work regardless of the obstacles. You become fixated on what you think is the only desirable choice.

The Defeatist Approach

When faced with a decision, you're immediately discouraged and expect the worst. Your discouragement can quickly turn into deep sadness. You may often say, "I give up." You may also berate yourself, believing that something is wrong with you and that things never work out for you.

Knowing your decision-making style (which may include more than one approach) can help you be more aware of your actions when faced with choices. It'll help you know what you need to do to make decisions in a way that will work better. Keep your style in mind as you read the rest of this chapter.

Acceptance, Again? Yes, Again.

You may believe that accepting you have a decision to make is automatic, but knowing and accepting are different. If you're ranting about the problem, complaining that it shouldn't have happened, or blaming someone for it, then you aren't accepting it. Part of accepting the problem is to see the issue as a natural part of life. After all, throughout your life you'll experience a need to solve problems and make difficult decisions.

Thoughts such as *I shouldn't have to deal with this* or *I can't think about this* get in the way of accepting the problem and moving forward. Intense resentment, sadness, anger, and fear about having to make a decision will interfere with effective thinking. Notice such thoughts and emotions, accept them, then bring yourself back to the facts of the situation and your options. If you must pull away for a brief period, do so wisely. Be mindful of how long a break you can take without negative consequences, such as losing a job or missing a social opportunity. Be clear as to how you'll use the break time to manage your emotions, so that you'll be calmer and able to make decisions in a more balanced way.

If you tend to use the Impulsive Approach to decision making, practicing mindfulness (see chapter 4) will help you develop a pause before acting. This means taking time to step back from your emotions and observe them, with awareness that you have an urge to act emotionally. When faced with a decision, practice waiting. If possible, pledge to *not* make a decision until a certain length of time has passed, no matter how strong your urge to do so. This will give you the opportunity to think more carefully and to practice sitting with the difficult feelings involved in decision making.

Mindfulness will also be helpful if you use the Dependent Approach to decision making. When you're mindful of your internal experience, you'll be more aware of your own preferences, as opposed to what someone else thinks. You may also benefit from working on your identity (see chapter 8). Knowing your values and goals will help guide you in making daily decisions. You might also give yourself more options to choose from. Consider asking multiple people for their opinions about your dilemma, including people who are likely to have different ideas. Then consider all the suggestions carefully to determine what you think is best. Making a list of pros and cons for each option may be particularly helpful.

If you use the Passive Approach to decision making, you may benefit from the ways of managing your emotions discussed in chapter 2. When faced with a decision, you may want to set a deadline for yourself. Pushing yourself to act despite your discomfort will be a worthwhile challenge. For routine decisions that don't involve significant consequences, such as where to go for dinner, maybe give yourself five minutes. If the decision is one that will have a larger impact on your life, such as whether to accept a job offer, then you might want to give yourself a day or two (as long as you won't miss any actual deadlines).

If you use the Willful Approach to decision making, one option is to write down past experiences when you've made decisions based on only what you desired. Any time you find yourself being willful in decision making, you can read what you've written to remind yourself of these experiences. Also, list the pros and cons of each of your options in a wholehearted way, really giving each option a fair consideration. Give thought to each option's likely consequences to your relationships and your view of yourself. When you find yourself being willful about an option that isn't likely to be successful or effective, consider why that option's so important to you. What do you stand to gain? Is there another way to get the result that matters to you? For example, if you want to live independently, maybe there are ways other than living in a particular apartment or with a certain person that would work. Sometimes, when you know what you want, you can find alternative ways to make it happen.

If you use the Overanalyzing Approach to decision making, you may want to give yourself deadlines for making decisions. Then put a reward in place for meeting that deadline, and perhaps a negative consequence if you don't make the decision on time. After you finalize your choice, use relaxation and distraction (see chapter 2) to manage your fears of not having made the perfect choice.

If you tend to use the Defeatist Approach to decision making, you probably think that you're flawed or that you do everything wrong and that's why you can't make decisions. Practice letting go of judgment (see chapter 6) so that you can focus on making effective decisions. You may also want to visualize yourself going successfully through the steps of making a decision.

The exercises in the rest of this chapter will help you learn decision-making skills. If you have an important, time-limited decision to make now, you may want to read through the material first and come back later to do each exercise. You may also find it helpful to review these ideas about decision making whenever you're faced with a choice in the future.

Separate the Decision from the Emotion

If you're emotionally sensitive, you may have difficulty making any decision that would lead to emotional pain. In this way, your emotions block you from putting your best decisions into action. For example, maybe the problem is you don't have enough money to pay your bills. Getting a new job is the solution that would work best. When you think about applying for jobs, however, you think, *I want to go to work, but I'm too afraid no one will hire me*. That statement includes both a solution (apply for jobs) and an emotional dilemma (you fear disappointment or shame if no one offers you a job). Defining the situation in that way keeps you paralyzed—you can't take the necessary action because you're too afraid of the emotional consequences. Emotions interwoven into problems are especially difficult for defeatist avoiders, who see problems as unsolvable anyway.

Fear of unwanted emotions obscures the fact you know what you want and need to do. In the example above, you want and need to get a job. That's the solution. The emotional challenge is coping with disappointment and other difficult emotions during your job search.

When faced with a difficult decision, ask yourself: *What am I trying to solve? What's my primary goal, and what's the emotion that gets in the way of that goal?* Separating the solution from the emotional challenge in this way will help you see the issues more clearly.

Let's say you want to break up with Joaquin, your boyfriend; you want to date other people. The statement "I don't want Joaquin to be angry with me and I want to date other people" is not a problem definition. That's the desired choice and your emotional dilemma rolled into one. This makes it look as though the problem has no solution, because it's likely you can't have things both ways. If you untangle the emotional dilemma from the problem, the solution will be clear, as will the challenge you face emotionally in putting the solution into action. In the example of wanting to break up with Joaquin, the desired outcome is dating other people. The emotional dilemma is that you don't want Joaquin to be angry with you. So your challenge in this case is really about managing your emotions so that you can cope with Joaquin being angry with you. Most solutions and decisions have emotional consequences, and willingness to cope with the emotions that come with the solutions is part of good decision making.

Accepting the emotional consequences of a decision is part of the decision-making and problem-solving process. Making a decision and being angry about the consequences will create ongoing misery. Sometimes it simply isn't possible to avoid undesired consequences.

Examining the Emotional Consequences

On the following worksheet (or a full-size version you download from http://www.newharbinger.com/29934), write a decision that you're considering making. (If you're currently faced with multiple decisions or many options, you can make copies of the worksheet, or just do this exercise in a journal or notebook.) Below the decision, list the positive and/or negative emotional consequences. For example, if you're considering quitting your job, an immediate consequence might be relief. A long-term one might be regret or sadness. Finally, based on the expected emotional consequences, write whether the decision would be an act of avoidance or an effective use of emotional information. If you're considering quitting a job you love because you made a mistake, that would be avoidant. You'll know the difference. When you're avoiding, you'll feel uneasy or anxious, perhaps overwhelmed. When you're using emotional information effectively, you might feel sadness, joy, or emotional pain about the decision.

When doing this exercise, follow the advice below that fits your decision-making style:

- *Overanalyzing Approach: Stop yourself from repeatedly going through a list of "what ifs." Focus on the facts you have now.*
- *Defeatist Approach: Notice your thoughts about the situation being hopeless, and keep working. Don't give up on the process. Take action on the decisions you listed.*
- *Impulsive Approach: Go through the exercise slowly and carefully. Take steps to cope with your anxiety so that you don't act without careful thought.*
- *Dependent Approach: Complete this exercise based only on what you think, not what someone else might think or say or what the "right" answer is. (Getting input later could be helpful, after you know more clearly what your own thoughts are.)*
- *Passive Approach: Give yourself deadlines, and push yourself to take action.*
- *Willful Approach: Practice considering all the options accurately and carefully. As an experiment, try choosing the option that makes the most factual sense, and try to imagine the outcome in detail.*

Emotional Consequences of Your Decision

Decision: ______________________________

Immediate Consequences

Positive: ______________________________

Negative: ______________________________

Long-Term Consequences

Positive: ______________________________

Negative: ______________________________

Is it avoidant or effective? ______________________________

Example

Decision: *I want to go back to school to finish my degree.*

Immediate Consequences

Positive: *I'd enjoy being with friends, I'd be proud of myself, my parents would be proud of me*

Negative: *I'd have to study, I'd be scared of failing, I'd be on a tight budget, I couldn't buy clothes I wanted or go out as much*

Long-Term Consequences

Positive: *I could have the job I really want and higher income, and think of myself as more accomplished; I could do more to help others*

Negative: *I'd have to pay more taxes, I'd have a more demanding work schedule*

Is it avoidant of effective? *Not going back to school is avoidant because going back to school is what I really want to do. I want to avoid the fear of failing and not having money to spend while in school. I need a plan to cope with the short-term challenges to get what I want in the long run.*

Review what you've written. For decisions that involve avoidance of negative or positive emotions in the short term but block you from what you want in the long term, create a plan to cope with the short-term challenges. In the case of making a mistake at work, you could call a friend for support, review the successes you've had at work to balance your view, and find ways to comfort yourself (see chapter 2). Some of the ideas discussed in the section on failure later in this chapter may be helpful. You could take responsibility for the error, find ways to make up for the mistake, or make a plan that shows how you'll go forward.

Improve on Either/Or Thinking

Emotionally sensitive people tend to think in absolute terms and keep choices restricted, such as going back to school versus not going back to school. Whenever you seem to be facing an either/or decision, consider other possible options. In the example just given, going to school part-time or applying for a new job might be other options that could meet your needs. Or maybe you'd prefer to spend your time and resources traveling or interning at a company that interests you. Because anxiety about a problem will narrow your ability to problem solve, try to keep your mind open and flexible. Remember to ask yourself what alternatives besides the two choices you are considering you might prefer (Heath and Heath 2013).

Either/or thinking also gets in your way when you evaluate the way you solved a problem. If you look at your actions as being either the "right" or the "wrong" choice, you can always find parts of your solution that weren't perfect. Any time you criticize your solution without considering the ways it worked, as well as the ways it didn't, you decrease your confidence in your problem-solving ability.

Expanding Your Options

On the following chart, or in a journal or notebook, list problems that you're working on. Then list the choices you're considering. Finally, list other options that you could also consider. For example, maybe you're considering whether or not to go with friends to a movie. Think about what your other options might be, such as going to the gym, visiting your family, or finishing your taxes. Although you're likely to have discouraging thoughts about one or more options, such as *That would take too long* or *I'm not smart enough to do that,* simply notice those thoughts and let them go, and don't rule out any options at this point. You can evaluate them more carefully at a later time.

Problem	Either/Or Choices	Alternative Options

Go back over the options in columns 2 and 3. Draw a line through any choices that really don't interest you, but not those choices that scare you or that you think you can't do. Rank the choices that are left in terms of your preferences. Then list pros and cons for each. Remember to stick with facts. This process will help you think more flexibly about the choices you have.

Make the Best Decision for Each Step in the Solution

Often, emotionally sensitive people see such a big picture of what it takes to carry out a decision that it seems impossible to go forward. For example, a freshman in college may think of all the years of medical school necessary to become a doctor and wonder how she'll ever make it through. That's like a seven-year-old wondering how he'll ever read *Moby Dick*. Just as you learned one letter of the alphabet at a time, big problems are solved and goals accomplished one step at a time.

Focusing on Small Steps

In a journal or notebook, or on a separate sheet of paper, write down a solution to a problem. Now list the steps in your solution. List each step separately and break it down as much as possible. Put the first step into action, and then take each step one at a time. You may need to revise the steps as you go. That doesn't mean the solution isn't working; it's normal to adjust your plan as you progress.

Sometimes, emotionally sensitive people don't want to have to take the necessary steps or deal with the stress involved in getting their desire. This is often particularly true for those who use the Impulsive Approach to decision making, such as Emily:

> Emily is currently unemployed. She has lost several jobs because of absences, which usually occurred after she was criticized or believed she was criticized by supervisors. She wants to earn a top management position, but her unwillingness to bear criticism from supervisors keeps her from building a career.

When you think about what you want in "big picture" terms, consider whether you're willing or able to complete the steps necessary for success. For example, if you want to start your own company, you'll need to have money to live on until your company is profitable. If you want to move out on your own, you'll need a way to pay rent, pay for the deposit, and maybe pay for transportation. Acknowledge the many small goals you may need to achieve in support of your larger goal (Nezu, Nezu, and D'Zurilla 2007).

Once you've made a decision, anticipate and prepare for obstacles at every step. Know that you may need extra time to deal with unforeseeable difficulties. Recognize that sometimes a decision may not work out, no matter how much thought you gave to it, and you'll need a backup option. Being flexible will help you be successful.

Coping with Failure

Though no one enjoys lack of success, if you're emotionally sensitive, you probably tend to take your failed decisions or actions to mean that *you're* a failure as a person. You may view any negative feedback from bosses, friends, and others as a personal rejection. That leads to the unpleasant experience of shame. In that case, it's no wonder you agonize over every decision you make. Perhaps in addition, you view your failures as permanent and due to your personal flaws, instead of seeing them as temporary and a natural part of learning. Given that outlook, of course you take minimal risks and give up easily, whether planning a birthday party, taking a class, choosing a vacation destination, or deciding what to cook for dinner.

Everyone fails at some point. The more goals you attempt, the more times you're likely to fail. Changing your thinking about failure will help you learn from your mistakes and become better at making decisions (Halliman 2010).

If you view failure as an opportunity to learn, you can recognize that when you attempt a task but don't succeed, you usually still gain new skills and a better understanding of the situation (Dweck 2006). Even learning that you can't do something is helpful, perhaps as a signal that you should change your goals. Or just think of bodybuilders, who build muscle strength by doing a weight-lifting exercise "to failure" (until they can't do any more repetitions).

Another way to cope with failure is to recognize your successes. Paying attention to your accomplishments will help you not judge yourself when you don't succeed. Be as specific as possible in what you want to accomplish, and define the steps toward your goal so that you'll know when you've achieved each one. Having a clear idea of what you're working toward, and of the steps along the way, will help you not give up when you're struggling. Reward yourself for achieving each step and for persevering. The rewards don't have to be expensive—they can be simple, such as a cup of your favorite coffee or a magazine you enjoy reading.

Learn to see yourself as capable of succeeding. One way to work on this is to picture yourself being successful. Create a detailed visualization of what success will be like for you. What will it look like when you've accomplished your goal? Consider writing down your vision of success. Go over that visualization several times a week.

Looking at Problem Solving as a Learning Experience

Commit to viewing problem solving and decision making as skills you can develop to improve your life and decrease your emotional pain. Create a chart with the following headings (or download it in full-scale form from http://www.newharbinger.com/29934).

Problem	Possible Solutions	Potential Outcomes	Solution to Try	Result	What I Learned/ Reward

For each problem you encounter this week, write as many different solutions as possible on the chart. Resist procrastinating, and think through each problem or decision. If you notice that you're judging yourself, let go of judgments (see chapter 6) and concentrate on the possible solutions. Go through each alternative and consider the potential outcomes. Choose a solution to try. If it doesn't work, then write what you learned from your experience. Remember to reward yourself for going through the process.

At the end of the week, look for patterns in the way you chose solutions and in the results you obtained. If you consistntly didn't get desired results, then evaluate whether you're choosing realistic solutions and whether you're thinking through the potential outcomes. Perhaps you're giving up before you put your solution fully into action, giving up when you encounter an obstacle, or giving only partial effort to being successful.

Putting It All Together

If you're emotionally sensitive, chances are you find it difficult to keep your emotions in check when making decisions. Simply having a decision to make may trigger difficult emotions. Knowing your usual style of decision making can help you find ways to manage the emotions that arise, so that you can make decisions more effectively and thoughtfully. Focusing on long-term positive emotional outcomes instead of going with whatever choice avoids emotional pain or makes you feel good in the short term will decrease your stress and increase your emotional peace.

Setting goals and solving problems effectively involves knowing what you want and what you value in life. This means being clear about your identity, the topic of the next chapter.

CHAPTER 8

Developing Your Identity

Many emotionally sensitive people are often unclear about what it means to have a sense of identity or how to develop one. Your personal identity (i.e., your sense of who you are, or your self-view) includes the distinctive, enduring characteristics that are part of your personality, such as your emotional sensitivity. It's partially based on the many social roles you no doubt occupy—such as husband, father, brother, and friend. It may also be partially based on the groups and culture you belong to, such as middle class and Irish. Values and morals that guide your choices in life, your friendships, and your career aspirations are all part of your identity as well.

Developing a solid sense of identity will help you not be overwhelmed by your feelings. Once you have a sense of who you are, your emotional reactions—particularly your reactions to interpersonal difficulties—will be less frequent and intense. You'll be less likely to see others' judgments and reactions as threats or as defining your worth. You won't be as fearful of being abandoned or rejected. You'll also be less likely to mask your feelings or be ashamed of your emotional reactions. Making decisions will be less overwhelming, because you'll be clear about what's important to you.

An inaccurate or unstable sense of identity can manifest in different ways. You may take on other people's emotions and struggles, unable to separate their experiences from yours. You may find yourself becoming angry or deeply sad by just talking with someone who's feeling that way. In addition, you might make decisions that are contradictory, don't fit your personality, or don't work well in the long run. You may make failed starts down many different paths in life, feeling as if you don't have a map to guide you. Your view of yourself may depend too much on how others view you. Perhaps you judge and define yourself as flawed and not normal to the point you hate yourself (for help letting go of such judgments, see chapter 6).

Understanding Your Identity Development

Your identity doesn't come to you wholly developed. You learn who you are from your experiences over time; to some extent, your identity is ever evolving. As a child, you began to develop your sense of yourself through awareness of your likes, dislikes, skills, and talents, as well as how other people regarded you.

However, emotionally sensitive children often don't receive accurate feedback about themselves because their caregivers don't understand their sensitivity or don't have the skills, such as the ability to understand the difficulty of certain tasks and situations so as to give accurate feedback (Linehan 1993). Maybe your family and friends were embarrassed by your emotions, so they encouraged you in one way or another to hide them. Maybe you were often told that you couldn't possibly be as upset as you were acting or that you were just trying to get your way. Perhaps your feelings were ignored.

The feedback you received may have been so negative that you came to see yourself—your real self—as unacceptable. Maybe you were told that you were too emotional, too weak, too needy, or simply "crazy." Even now, you may be fearful of knowing yourself or experience such shame about who you think you are that it's painful to think about it. Take a deep breath, and let's look at what is and isn't true about who you are.

Myths vs. Facts About Who You Are

You may have grown up with other people's views of your behavior or character ingrained in your mind. You may not even be aware that some thoughts you have about yourself originally came from other people and have no basis in fact. If you see yourself as a burden, maybe that idea came from caregivers or significant people in your life who had little to give or were overwhelmed with their own lives. Maybe, in other words, that view was more about them than it was about you. Perhaps your family believed that showing emotions meant you were weak or that not getting a good grade meant that you were stupid. Every family has its own issues, and such misperceptions are common.

Myths may also come from your experiences. For example, if you weren't skilled in softball or soccer when you were a child, you may have decided that you don't have the ability to do any physical activities well. If your family was sports oriented, that could have led to other negative myths about yourself, such as that you don't know how to have fun. While it's true you weren't a top soccer player, you might have done well in other physical activities. Maybe you weren't athletic but had fun in other ways.

Identifying Myths About Who You Are

Place a check mark in the space next to any of the following statements that you agree with. At the end of the list, write any other negative beliefs you have about yourself.

____ 1. I'm a burden to others.

____ 2. I'm a flawed human being, and I can't let others know or I'll be cast out of society.

____ 3. If I speak up for myself, I'll be alone.

____ 4. I must always put others first. That's my role.

____ 5. I don't fit in society.

____ 6. I need someone to take care of me emotionally.

____ 7. I have to be in a romantic relationship or I can't survive.

____ 8. I'm weak because I have intense emotions.

____

____

These are all myths. In the exercises to come, you'll practice changing these myths to facts.

Changing Myths About Who You Are

Your beliefs about yourself affect the way you live your life. As long as your beliefs are accurate, they help you make decisions about what situations will be helpful, understand what circumstances might be challenging, predict how people will react to you, and determine what activities you might enjoy. If your beliefs about yourself aren't accurate, you may be confused by how other people see you. That lack of helpful knowledge about yourself makes it harder to manage your emotions.

People in general have a tendency to see only the evidence that supports their beliefs and discount any evidence to the contrary (McRaney 2011). That's one reason we often continue to accept myths.

Debunking Your Myths

Using the myths that you marked in the exercise above, try an experiment. Actively search for information that tells you the opposite of what you believe. If you marked the first myth, for example, look for ways you're *not* a burden to others. Really think hard and honestly about it, and don't discount yourself. Consider ways that you contribute to others' lives. Ask people whom you trust what *they* believe. If you marked myth 2, 3, 7, or 8, look for examples among people in the news or in your community that might disprove this myth—many people have acknowledged their flaws without being ostracized by society. Now go back and reword the myths to better reflect the truth and help you have a more accurate sense of yourself. For example, "I have to be in a romantic relationship or I can't survive" could be reworded to "I want to be in a romantic relationship so badly that sometimes I think I can't survive without it." Remember that accepting the truth doesn't mean you're giving in, settling, or working any less diligently to lessen your pain and have what you want in life.

Sometimes myths or false beliefs about yourself are based on old behaviors. Perhaps when you were younger you acted impulsively and did things you regretted, such as running away or verbally exploding. Maybe now you're more careful in your decisions and don't engage in such impulsive behaviors anymore. If you still think of yourself as someone who's impulsive even though you no longer act that way, then your view of yourself is out of date. Consider the myths that you identified above. Are any of those myths based on your past and not on the present?

You may also believe myths about yourself that are based on one or two isolated incidents. While you may have lied repeatedly about your activities to a boyfriend a few years ago, there's no reason to see yourself as a liar if you haven't repeated that behavior consistently in your relationships. At the same time, most people do have patterns of behavior that they aren't proud of and that have negative consequences. If you tend to engage in such behaviors, then changing those destructive patterns is important. Use the following exercise to consider patterns of unhelpful behavior that reflect ways you view yourself that affect your choices and decisions.

Your Story

Write out a description of the major events in your life through the years. Include significant mistakes, successes, and life events and what you learned from each. Illustrate your weaknesses and strengths. Think about the overall theme of your life. Possible themes are overcoming obstacles, loss, survival, empowerment, compassion, shame, struggle, chaos, success, contentment, and loyalty.

Go over what you've written, highlighting any patterns that you notice. The patterns will likely be related to the theme. In your story, what role do you typically have? Are you the hero? The villain? The victim? Are you the star of your own story, or is someone else the main focus?

If you're not the star or hero, rewrite your story from a perspective in which you are, while still sticking to facts. How did you survive tough situations? Make the theme of the story a positive one. How is it different? Perhaps the emotional tone of the story changes or the way you describe yourself is different. Maybe you notice outcomes you didn't see previously. If you struggle to find a way to rewrite the story, it may be because myths about your role in life have become part of your core beliefs about yourself and it's difficult to see the story in any other way. In this case, ask a trusted friend to help you with the rewrite. Remember that the story doesn't need to change to a pleasant one—you just want it to reflect whatever strengths and positives were evident in you or developed as a result.

Stereotypes

Another way of understanding the power of others' beliefs on your behavior is through the studies that have been done about stereotypes. Stereotypes are like myths that a lot of people believe about individuals with a common characteristic or a certain way of doing things.

In the 1960s, Robert Rosenthal and Lenore Jacobson (1963) administered a test to all students in an elementary school. They then told the teachers that based on the test results, some students were particularly likely to excel academically in the upcoming year, whereas others weren't.

The students to be identified as "gifted" were actually chosen at random, not by their performance on the test. At the end of the year, however, these students scored significantly higher on an IQ test than the other students.

That's an amazing result. The students themselves didn't know they had been designated as high achievers, and neither did their parents. Only the teachers knew. Thus the researchers concluded that the teachers' expectations caused the teachers to act in ways that improved the performance of the students who had been labeled as bright.

Other people's expectations affect both the way they treat you and the way you behave. Stereotypes are a form of expectations (Steele 2010). In general, the stereotype of emotionally sensitive people is that they're wimpy, touchy-feely, unstable, weak, unreliable, a pushover, overreactive, high maintenance, and less professional than those who aren't viewed as emotionally sensitive. This stereotype can affect the way you see yourself, as well as your performance in situations in which others have that view of you.

Any time you think that you're being judged by the emotionally sensitive stereotype, you may be afraid of showing "too much" emotion, which would have negative consequences for your relationships and/or your career. Guarding against emotions, however, takes away from the energy and concentration you have to devote to your job or to the people you're interacting with.

The added tension from the worry about being labeled will make it even more difficult to manage your emotions. The more you care, the more frustrated you'll be. The higher the stakes for your performance, the more panicked you'll likely be (Steele 2010).

You may go to work each day determined to not show emotion and fearful of others labeling you in a negative way. Maybe sometimes you go to work fearful that you'll cry, perhaps because you're angry with someone. You fear that if you cry, you'll be judged as unprofessional or weak. Your fears and worries make your job more tiring and difficult. As a result, you're actually more likely to cry. If this goes on for a long time, you may view yourself as a less competent employee and your ability to do your job well will diminish. Maybe you aren't even sure what would happen if you cried at work, but the fear is still there. Even if you're uncertain that anything negative would happen if you were labeled "emotionally sensitive," you only have to believe that something negative *could* happen (Steele 2010).

So what can you do? In situations in which you're worried about being stereotyped for your emotional sensitivity, you might decide to hold your head up and say, "Yes, I'm emotionally sensitive, so I'll be back as soon as I wipe a few tears away." Or you can use humor to defuse the situation, such as smiling and saying, "No, I'm too emotionally sensitive to watch cartoons, much less reality shows." If you're comfortable with your sensitivity, others are more likely to be as well. Practice accepting yourself even when others don't.

There may be situations in which you can't be open about your emotional sensitivity. When that's the case, be diligent about using strategies to regulate your emotions and keep yourself as relaxed as possible. Lowering your overall tension level will help. See chapter 2 for ideas on relaxation and general ways to manage emotions, and see chapter 3 for advice about self-care. Not judging yourself (chapter 6) and practicing mindfulness (chapter 4) will also be helpful. Finally, remind yourself of ways the "emotionally sensitive" stereotype isn't accurate—for example, think of great leaders who were emotionally sensitive or of characteristics you possess that show the stereotype is not accurate (Steele 2010).

Roles That Keep You Trapped

The roles you occupy in relation to other people are part of your identity. You probably have a role with your family members and friends as "the emotionally sensitive one." More specifically, you may be seen as "the caring one," "the listening one," or "the one who will always help." You may also be "the one who overreacts" or "the one who's too fragile to hear difficult information."

Whatever your role is, your role affects your identity. When your family expects you to react in certain ways, there's usually a strong pull to do just that. In addition, your role will affect how others treat you. If you're "the listening one," others may not realize that sometimes you'd like to talk too. If you're seen as too fragile, others may keep secrets from you or not tell you the truth. If they see you as "the quiet one," they may not ask for your input.

Your family members and friends may not really listen to your complaints or hurt feelings, attributing all your negative emotional reactions to your emotional sensitivity, even when your reactions are the same as those who aren't emotionally sensitive. Instead of saying "I'm sorry you're upset about your friend moving," for example, someone may ask, "You're not going all drama queen on me again, are you?" This is unfair, to say the least, but you can do something about it.

Redefining Your Roles

To understand more about how others' expectations affect your behavior, write down a description of your role in your family. You can do this in a journal or notebook, or simply on a separate sheet of paper. Then write down a description of your role in relation to your closest friends.

Be sure to include how your behavior contributes to the role you have. How does your role affect your relationship with each person? What do you enjoy about your role, and what doesn't work for you?

Read what you've written. Now write what you'd like to change about your role with your family and your role with your friends. How would you need to behave differently in order to change your role?

For example, let's say that you want to be seen as someone who can listen without becoming upset. You want to change your role with your friends from being "the person who overreacts" to "someone who's a good listener." You realize that whenever people talk with you about their issues, you tend to get tense, worry about all the awful things that could result, and then judge yourself for overreacting. Your plan might include practicing relaxation exercises to reduce your tension. Practicing mindfulness every day could help you stay in the moment and not think ahead to awful things that could happen. You could also practice mindful listening and not judging.

Make a plan for how to change your role. Choose only one or two changes to make at a time. List specifically what skills you'll use to behave in a new way.

Track your progress. This can be as simple as checking off whether you practiced a skill, such as mindful listening, on your calendar each day. Give yourself a reward for practicing, such as a compliment for persevering. You can slowly add more skills to practice as you go along. Though it may take some time, people will notice the changes you're making and view you in a new way. When they do, their expectations will change, and you'll find it easier to use your new skills.

Emptiness and Identity

Not everyone who's emotionally sensitive experiences emptiness in terms of their identity, and those who do may not all experience it the same way. One emotionally sensitive person described emptiness as being "like a cold shell, a shell of a person with no insides, nothing there. It feels like you cannot breathe and you have nowhere to go for refuge. Suffocating." Another emotionally sensitive person described emptiness as "not knowing how you're feeling, or feeling nothing or not knowing what you want in life, leaves you with a dark empty pit, especially in the stomach and mind. Emptiness is a void. Nothing matters and you wouldn't know what to feel…if you could even feel anything in the first place. It consumes you, and nothing and no one can fill that void…."

Emptiness of identity seems to be not knowing who you are, what you feel, or what you want. It's a hollow feeling, a nothingness. It's as if you're a puppet just responding to what's expected or what string is pulled.

There's a discomfort in emptiness that leads some people to seek pain. Others try to fill the emptiness with drugs, alcohol, work, food, or other compulsive behavior. Some become overly dependent on another person. In fact, many who experience emptiness of identity find some comfort by being around others and taking on a pseudo-identity that fits the group they're with. If you tend to do this, you may panic when you aren't around people, because then the emptiness is evident again, and you're back to having little sense of how to be or what to do.

Filling the emptiness means building your identity, finding meaning, contributing, and connecting with life and with others. Mindfulness is a way to begin (see chapter 4). Through mindfulness, you can focus on being present and developing a sense of your own thoughts and your own preferences by paying attention to your thoughts and feelings. What's your favorite color? Which restaurant would you prefer for dinner with friends? How would you choose to spend a free afternoon if you could do whatever you wanted? Experiment to find answers to these questions if you don't know them. Try different activities to discover how you most enjoy spending your time. Allocate some time to considering your spirituality. What do you believe? Maybe you'd like to learn more about different spiritual philosophies.

Pay attention to your values in life. What are your top values? Practice naming three different things you're grateful for each day to help identify what you value. Be mindful of the ways you contribute to others. Maybe you're a good listener, or maybe you cheer people up with your gift of humor. Perhaps you regularly help others overcome obstacles or you readily offer love and compassion. Maybe those behaviors point to what you value.

If your habit has been to attempt to hide from the emptiness by being with others, do some activities independently. Allow yourself to spend brief periods of time alone, tolerating the discomfort that you'll initially feel. Working to accept and fill the emptiness rather than avoiding it will, over time, lead to a more peaceful and rewarding life.

Giving Up Self-Hatred and Building Your Identity

Many emotionally sensitive people seem to dislike or even hate themselves. The reasons for this vary but seem to fall into certain categories: self-blame, accepting stereotypes, having self-constructs that aren't accurate, not living a life that's consistent with your values, treating yourself as if you don't matter, and having to live with the pain that comes with emotional sensitivity. Changing self-hatred is a complex challenge.

Stop Blaming Yourself

Blaming yourself for things that turned out badly is different from taking responsibility for them. When you take responsibility, you simply acknowledge the facts about your part in what happened. Blaming yourself is more negative and self-accusatory.

If you're emotionally sensitive, you may often blame yourself when things go wrong. You allow yourself little room for error. Often the blame you place on yourself is based simply on the fact that something negative happened, rather than on an evaluation of *how* it happened. For example, if your daughter is angry, you think it's because you must have spoken too harshly to her or done something awful. If your boss rejects the report from your work group, it's because you did a horrible job writing it. These are possible explanations, but they're not necessarily true. There could be other explanations.

All-or-nothing thinking, as well as perfectionism, can increase the frequency and severity of your self-blame. If you focus on what doesn't work, and you blame yourself for most of the negative events that occur in your life, you'll have a negative view of yourself that will contribute to overwhelming and upsetting emotions. For example, if your boss asks you to revise one paragraph of a report, you may decide you totally messed up the assignment.

You may go even further and decide that unfortunate outcomes are due to your character flaws. In the example just presented, you might decide you messed up the assignment because you can't do anything right. Blaming negative outcomes on character flaws is an example of *fundamental attribution error.*

Fundamental attribution error (Ross 1977) is the tendency to use personality-based explanations for behavior that's better explained by circumstances. For example, perhaps you have a really tiring week in which you get home late each evening, and then at the end of the week you berate yourself for being a lazy bum who doesn't even wash the dishes. The reason you didn't do the dishes was because you were exhausted, not because you're lazy. You could develop a long list of personality flaws for yourself in this way, not to mention a ton of negative judgments and dislike—none of it based on truth.

Understanding the situation as the reason for your behavior is different from making excuses. In the example above, it's simply not logical to expect yourself to function at the same speed and accomplish the same amount of work when you're tired as when you're well rested. Looking at the facts will help you accept the truth of the situation and result in a more accurate view of who you are.

Stop Over-Apologizing

The emotionally sensitive, especially those who want to please others, are often champion apologizers. You may apologize frequently, because you care about others' feelings and because you don't want anyone to be angry or upset with you. *So what's the problem?* you may be thinking. *We could use more politeness in this world, right?* Of course, apologizing when you've done something to be sorry for is admirable. But perhaps you've walked into a room, bumped into an empty chair, and said, "Oh, excuse me." Or apologized because it was raining. Or because someone else was sick. When you routinely apologize for these kinds of things, you portray yourself as responsible for all sorts of problems and accountable to everyone and everything, even inanimate objects (like the empty chair). Perhaps you often apologize for your opinions and ideas or apologize for standing up for yourself. When you do, you display a lack of self-respect that influences others to hold you in low regard. As a result, people may see you as inadequate, powerless, or incompetent. They may be less likely to take you seriously or even listen to what you have to say (Linehan 1993). Acting in ways that don't show self-respect may increase your dislike of yourself, as well.

Sometimes the emotionally sensitive are plagued with fears about relationships they treasure. Apologies can be an indirect request for reassurance, particularly when you allow others to define your value as a person. To cope with your fears, you may apologize to your loved ones frequently, perhaps even unaware that you're hoping for the other person to reassure you or tell you that there's no reason to apologize. Such behavior, however, can cause others to become resentful, thus damaging the relationships you treasure so much.

OVER-APOLOGIZING CAN CLOUD YOUR UNDERSTANDING OF YOURSELF

When you apologize too often, you may lose your sense of what you're truly feeling, because your focus is always on other people's reactions. You may not consider your motivations, how the issues you're apologizing for came about, or even whether you were really at fault. You may apologize automatically, just to placate people. If you stop over-apologizing, then your feelings, values, and beliefs will become more clear, helping you maintain or develop your sense of who you are.

OVER-APOLOGIZING DAMAGES RELATIONSHIPS

Apologizing too frequently could be robbing you of authentic relationships and feedback by limiting discussion of the true issues and preventing constructive conflict. If you aren't expressing your authentic feelings, the other person probably isn't comfortable doing so either. You're losing the trust and intimacy that might come from sharing thoughts and feelings as you work toward understanding each other's views. Plus you're missing out on what's happening with your friends and families.

Over-apologizing may cause your friends to see you as too fragile for honesty. They may reserve their true feelings and opinions because they believe you can't handle those truths. As a result, you may not be getting accurate feedback about the way your friends perceive you. Some friends may even see the relationship as too difficult and pull away.

Over-apologizing may also give the impression that you think people should apologize for any possible insult, no matter how small—in other words, that you can't let anything go. Your friends who are more easygoing may find that interactions with you are tense because you seem to worry too much. They may wonder whether you're "keeping score" and expecting them to apologize for things they normally wouldn't. This may create pressure for them to act a certain way, which results in awkward interactions.

Finally, over-apologizing can make it seem as if you think every situation is about *you*, which is ironic given that what drives your apologetic behavior is concern for other people's feelings.

APOLOGIZE WITH AWARENESS

Sometimes, to save an important relationship, you may apologize even though you did nothing wrong. If you find yourself doing this repeatedly with the same person, you might want to take a closer look at that relationship. Relationships that depend on you always being "wrong" or giving up your own needs and feelings aren't healthy.

If the relationship is a good one and you rarely need to apologize just to save it, then consider the pros and cons of doing so. The costs of apologizing even though you don't think you were wrong may not be as high as the costs of losing a good relationship. In this case, you might want to apologize, with the greater good—the good of the relationship—in mind.

Learning to apologize only when it's appropriate could improve your self-respect, your awareness of your own opinions, your acceptance by others, and your overall understanding of your identity. Awareness is the first step. Be mindful of how often you apologize when there's no reason for it. Consider counting the number of unjustified apologies you give in a day. Notice whether there are certain situations that you're more likely to apologize for or certain people (or types of people) to whom you're more likely to apologize. Sometimes just noticing your behavior will influence you to make different choices.

Next, decide what words (in general) you might use instead of an apology. One option is to comment on the other person's experience—for example, "That must have been sad"—instead of saying "I'm so sorry."

Live a Life That's Consistent with Your Values

It may often seem there isn't enough time to think about living with meaning or putting your energy into what you believe in. From the moment you wake up in the morning, you've got tasks to do. You probably give little thought to whether or not your time is spent in ways that are consistent with your values. Maybe you complete one task after another all day long, then fall into bed exhausted.

Living consistently with your values is important to the way you see yourself as well as to reducing your stress. Part of your self-view comes from what you do—how you behave. When you live inconsistently with your values, you may be generally dissatisfied with your life and see it as lacking meaning (Wilson and DuFrene 2010). Or maybe you hate your life because it doesn't fit the way you truly want to live. If you value family, yet you spend most of your time away from your family, you can expect to feel emotional distress. If you value honesty, and you're lying about important issues in your life, that will impact your view of yourself.

Many emotionally sensitive people say they don't know what their values are. And it's obviously difficult to live a life that's consistent with your values when you don't know what they are. Although you can probably easily identify many values you hold, such as honesty, family, and service to others, figuring out which ones are most important to you is likely to be harder.

Getting Closer to Your Values

Place a check mark next to the following values that are most important to you. Choose no more than ten.

____ Acceptance and equality ____ Accomplishment

____ Adventure ____ Beauty

____ Community ____ Creativity

____ Discipline ____ Family

____ Flexibility ____ Friendships

____ Fun ____ Generosity

____ Gratitude

____ Hard work

____ Health

____ Helping others

____ Independence

____ Making a difference

____ Openness

____ Privacy

____ Reliability

____ Safety

____ Service to others

____ Spirituality

____ Security

____ Teamwork

____ Tolerance

____ Tradition

____ Truth and honor

____ Wealth

Out of these ten, choose the five values that are most important to you. Now narrow that list to three. Are these your top three values in life? If not, what are your top three values? Write them below.

1. ______________________________

2. ______________________________

3. ______________________________

Over the next few days, think about ways you might change your routine so that your daily life is more consistent with your top values. Try to come up with at least two things you can do that are in line with each value. Think in terms of small steps that you can take right now. Be specific. If one of your values is to nurture friendships, then you might plan to call friends or invite them to spend time with you. Be sure the plan is one that you can control. For example, you can make sure you invite friends; you can't be sure they'll accept.

Value: ______________________________

What I Can Do to Live a Life That's Consistent with This Value This Week

1. ______________________________

2. ______________________________

3. ______________________________

Value: ______________________________

What I Can Do to Live a Life That's Consistent with This Value This Week

1. ______________________________

2. ______________________________

3. ______________________________

Value: ______________________________

What I Can Do to Live a Life That's Consistent with This Value This Week

1. ______________________________

2. ______________________________

3. ______________________________

Start date: ______________

Now write tomorrow's date as your start date, and put your values into practice over the coming week. At the end of that week, check whether you put each value into practice in all the ways you listed. Once you've made these changes, notice your stress level and your view of yourself and your life. Did they improve?

Repeat this exercise with different ways of practicing your values to help you get closer to living a values-based life.

Practice Self-Validation

Self-validation is critical for living with intense emotions, forming healthy relationships, and thriving. Self-validation means acknowledging and accepting your internal experience and behavior as making sense and being understandable either in general or in the context of your life. For example, if you're angry because someone purposefully scratched your new car, it's easy to validate your anger, because anyone would feel angry in that situation. If you're emotionally sensitive, however, it's likely that you're sometimes upset by things that don't seem to bother others. When this occurs, you can validate your feelings by saying, "I'm emotionally sensitive, so it's understandable that I'm distressed about this, though others may not be." In this way, you don't judge yourself.

Validation lowers the intensity of emotions (Linehan 1993). Validating yourself when you're experiencing strong emotions will help you accept yourself and learn to trust your inner experiences, which will lead to a stronger sense of identity.

There are six levels of validation (Linehan 1993). You can apply these levels to self-validation. With practice and more practice, you'll begin to self-validate automatically.

Level 1: Being present. To be present means to ground yourself and not dissociate from, suppress, or numb your emotions. Be mindful of your emotions and thoughts. Listen to your internal experience—when you do, you confirm that you matter and that your internal experience has value. Working on being present may require the assistance of a therapist (see chapter 4).

Level 2: Accurate reflection. Acknowledge your internal state to yourself. Observe it and think about how you might describe it. Reflect on what triggered the emotion. Reflect on the ways you feel the emotion in your body.

When you observe and describe your internal experience, you don't interpret, judge, or make assumptions. You just notice what's there and the facts surrounding it. For example: "I feel angry, and it started yesterday after my friend canceled lunch. I sense tightness in my stomach and heat on my face. Ah, I feel fear as well." Stating what you can observe about your experience helps you build trust in your internal experience and your understanding of who you are.

Level 3: Guessing. Sometimes you won't be sure what you're feeling or thinking. In these situations, you may want to say something like "If someone else were in this situation, they'd probably feel sad. Am I sad?" Look for clues to what you're feeling in the actions you want to take (Linehan 1993). For example, if you want to hide, maybe you're feeling shame. Maybe you're thinking shameful thoughts. Notice where you feel body sensations, and consider whether these sensations fit with a particular emotion—for example, fear is often felt as a tightening in the throat. If you're feeling fear, maybe you're thinking scary thoughts. Guessing your emotions and thoughts based on the information you have will help you learn more about yourself.

Level 4: Validating by history. Sometimes you'll have thoughts and feelings that are based on previous events. Maybe when people argue you get scared, because past arguments led to your being hurt. In this case, you can validate yourself by saying, "It's acceptable and understandable that I'm afraid when people argue, because in the past that situation has been dangerous for me," which takes into account those past experiences that influence your current reactions.

Level 5: Normalizing. Sometimes people who have intense emotions don't see any of their emotional reactions as being normal. It's important to validate yourself when what you feel is the same as what anyone would feel. If you're sad because you didn't get a job you wanted, remember that others would be sad if that happened to them. Ask yourself whether what you're feeling is what most other people would experience, and validate those feelings as such.

Level 6: Radical genuineness. In terms of self-validation, radical genuineness means being your real self and not lying to yourself. It means not pretending to be someone you aren't.

Putting It All Together

Issues with identity seem to abound for emotionally sensitive people. Hopefully, by putting the ideas in this chapter into practice, you've already begun to find your identity becoming more clear and stable. Now that you have a more accurate and stable sense of your identity, and now that you have skills to manage intense emotions, you're ready to look at forming and improving relationships. Developing and maintaining supportive relationships will prove very useful in those times when your emotions threaten to overwhelm you.

CHAPTER 9

Living with or Overcoming Loneliness

Relationships can be a source of joy and help add meaning to your life. If you're emotionally sensitive, friends and loved ones can provide you with companionship and assistance during difficult times (as well as share in your celebrations), broaden your perspective, and offer feedback that will help you understand yourself.

Relationships are also important to helping you manage your emotions, in many different ways:

- Listening to others' descriptions of emotional experiences can teach you to label your own experiences accurately, especially if you were never taught this.
- Knowing that other people feel the same emotions as you (though perhaps not as intensely) can help you not judge your feelings.
- Sharing your joy with others may magnify your pleasure, while sharing your sadness can lessen your pain.
- When you're angry or ashamed, talking openly with someone you trust can help ease that feeling.

- Learning how others solved problems may give you hope that you can do the same.
- It may be easier to overcome fear of certain situations or of new experiences if you have a "buddy" with you.

On the other hand, relationships are full of emotional landmines. Yet whether you're unsure how to form relationships, struggle with out-of-balance relationships, or have given up on relationships, it's likely that deep in your heart you crave a sense of connection and belonging.

Loneliness

Many emotionally sensitive people tend to feel intense loneliness on a recurring basis. Perhaps routine interactions with people at work or school keep you from feeling lonely some of the time, but then it hits you in the evening, when you sit at home wishing you could tell someone about your day. Perhaps weekends when you don't have plans with anyone are particularly lonely. Holidays and your birthday may be the most painful times of all, if you can't share them with friends and loved ones. Maybe you're lonely every day.

Why You Can't Just "Make Friends"

The obvious solution to loneliness is to make friends. However, while loneliness is painful, the thought of attempting to meet people can be even more agonizing. Being told to just "make friends," as if it were easy to do, can lead to increased self-hatred and doubt.

Often the difficulty in meeting people is about fear of rejection and being judged. Rejection, even by strangers, can hurt you to the core. The region of the brain that's activated when you experience rejection is the same that registers emotional responses to physical pain (Kross et al. 2011). In fact, the thought of people you hardly know having the power to hurt you deeply may be particularly scary. Or maybe you believe there's something profoundly wrong with you—perhaps that you're basically unlovable—and that this flaw is obvious to others. You wouldn't want to risk the pain of having that belief confirmed by being shunned. You may also be afraid that you'll be seen as weird, an outcast, or troubled—even dangerous—because you have few or no friends.

Plenty of People Are Lonely

Part of loneliness is thinking you're the only one who feels that way. Actually, many people suffer from loneliness. Even though you may feel the pain of loneliness more intensely and more often than others, everyone feels lonely sometimes.

There may be an evolutionary reason that loneliness is such a common feeling. It prompts you to pay attention to relationships, which until relatively recently in human history were critical for survival. While being a member of a "tribe" is no longer necessary for our physical well-being, the fact is that having friends and feeling as though we belong to a community still enhances our emotional health.

The Consequences of Loneliness

The consequences of chronic loneliness are significant. If you're frequently lonely, your difficulties in life will seem worse, and your joys will be minimized. If you already struggle to cope with difficult emotions, loneliness can add significantly to your emotional distress. In addition to the emotional pain, chronic loneliness impairs your concentration and attention and contributes to premature aging and even death (Cacioppo and Patrick 2008).

Examining the Causes of Your Loneliness

Just as loneliness can be painful, so can relationships—as anyone who has fought with a friend or suffered a breakup knows. Thus, deciding how to deal with loneliness requires careful thought. Maybe you think that being lonely is preferable to risking friendships. Before you decide that's your best option, though, ask yourself whether your decision to not connect with others is based on fear, such as fear of others criticizing you, rather than your true preferences. If it's fear-based, it may be blocking you from living a life that's consistent with your values. Taking action to build relationships may be one more way to live a values-based life (see chapter 8) and thereby reduce your emotional distress.

Think about what else may be preventing you from building relationships. Is it a judgmental belief, such as that you're basically unlikable or that people are out to hurt you? If so, remember that judgments typically represent inaccurate overgeneralizations. If you're open to a different view, you can probably find evidence in your life that contradicts that belief. For example, while people may have purposefully hurt you, it's probably not true of everyone in your life. Very likely only some people have behaved in ways that hurt you, either intentionally or unintentionally. Remember, too, that there are all different kinds of people. If one person wasn't a good friend to you, another may be. If you weren't a good friend to someone, keep in mind that your future behavior doesn't have to be the same.

Finally, maybe your decision to stay lonely is based on problems you can resolve. If you don't have the social skills needed to make friends, for example, it might help to take a class or talk to a therapist. If you're hypersensitive to routine comments, then learning ways to cope with the give-and-take of friendly conversations might be the answer. If you've typically chosen to have relationships with verbally abusive people, then you may need to learn how to choose friends who are respectful to you. If you're not willing to work on friendships because you don't have the energy or care enough about yourself, then seeking treatment for depression might be called for. Understanding what you have to overcome in order to meet people and build friendships will help you make an informed decision about whether you're ready to start the process.

If you're not willing to work on relationships, you can still learn to not judge yourself for being lonely, as well as build other kinds of meaningful connections to minimize the pain of the loneliness you experience.

Stop Judging Your Loneliness

When you're lonely, you may have judgmental thoughts, such as *I don't have any friends to hang out with—I'm such a loser.* As you know from chapter 6, judging yourself in this way adds to your emotional discomfort and makes coping with a tough situation even more difficult. Letting go of such judgments won't take away all the pain of loneliness, but it'll help significantly. Accept your loneliness as a fact but only a part of your life, like a spot in your yard where the grass doesn't grow as thickly. You'd prefer to have your lawn be lush all over, but having a sparse patch doesn't mean you can't have an attractive yard. In the same way, having loneliness doesn't mean you can't lead a contented life. You can focus on other ways to enhance your life, such as those discussed next. If you don't accept the loneliness that's there, or work on changing it, then you'll continue to suffer.

Alternative Ways to Experience a Sense of Connection

You can connect to life through activities you enjoy (Page and Rhodes 2012), which may be as simple as gardening, reading, or taking walks. Try to do these things mindfully (see chapter 4). Total absorption in an activity will help create a sense of belonging and connectedness. If you find your thoughts wandering or find yourself making judgments (like *I'm a loser, these plants will never grow, and this won't make a difference anyway*)—which is normal—simply redirect your attention to the activity at hand. Be mindful of the physical sensations involved in whatever you're doing. For example, if you're gardening, then completely focus on the feel of the earth, the smells, and the breeze on your face. The more you focus on the activity and let go of judgmental thoughts, the more enjoyable and rewarding the experience will be.

Immerse yourself in creative activities (Page and Rhodes 2012). Paint, write, cook, create photos or films, decorate, play music, arrange flowers, or spend time in art museums. Do whatever is your creative passion. An artistic connection can lead to feeling more alive and part of the world.

Some people experience a sense of connection through dedication to a cause or providing service to others. Your cause may be related to the work you do, but not necessarily. Perhaps you want to feed the hungry or work for human rights. Find a way to be involved in making a difference. (Watch for extreme thinking that can stop you from even getting started with this, such as *This problem is too big.* Making one small difference is enough.) You can also help others through online volunteer work and not leave your home. There are websites for online volunteer opportunities that might fit you, such as http://www.volunteermatch.org.

Being lonely doesn't mean you need to be isolated. Engage with the world. Consider doing by yourself the things you'd like to do if you had friends or companions. Going out to dinner and to movies by yourself can be daunting, but you'll find it easier over time. As discussed in chapter 1, emotionally sensitive people often feel a connection to the world through nature. Go to a park or lake, or walk in an arboretum.

Studying history is a way to gain a sense of connection with the past. Traveling to historic places, such as walking down the same road Cleopatra is believed to have walked or visiting sites of the early American colonies, can enhance that sense of being a part of humanity. Working with your own family history and genealogy can forge an even more personal connection to past and present generations. Understanding your ancestry may help you learn more about yourself.

Consider focusing on your spirituality. Whatever your beliefs, being in touch with a higher power can be comforting. A sense of greater meaning carries with it a sense of connection.

Pets can be wonderful companions. Maybe you'd like to adopt a cat or dog. You can also volunteer to care for animals at a shelter or provide them with a foster home.

Consider a pen pal. Writing a person who lives in a different country could be a safe and interesting way to build a connection to someone.

Perhaps you found yourself dismissing these ideas as you looked over them. What you really want might be lots of friends who accept and love you and never hurt you. You may wonder how something like building a relationship with a pen pal can make a dent in your feelings of loneliness. Watch out for extreme thinking, such as *This will never work.* Following the suggestions in this section won't erase your loneliness, but it'll help. Try one, give it your full attention, and you'll see a difference. Then try another one. If you still wish to spend more time closer to people, then classes, book clubs, or other group activities can offer you a structured and relatively nonthreatening way to start.

Getting Ready to Make Connections with People

If you've decided you want to build relationships, you need to make yourself open and available to interact with others. That means being around people, so that you have the opportunity to connect.

Change Your Relationship to Electronics

Television, computers, and smartphones may partially fill people's emotional needs for belonging and friendship. If having a favorite television show or online game alleviates the pain of loneliness, then that could be positive in the short run. But easing the pain of loneliness through technology may take away your motivation to find face-to-face relationships, with the result that in a time of deep need, there may be no one in your life.

Television shows, games on your phone, and other forms of entertainment are better used as tools to connect with people. Perhaps a certain show is a popular topic of conversation at your work. By watching that show, you can join the conversation. Perhaps you might invite people over to watch it with you. That would be different than using television to avoid or substitute for personal relationships.

Whenever you're around people, put the electronics down and try being mindfully present. Focus on what other people are doing and saying, not on yourself. Be curious about the people around you. Remember to let go of judgments (see chapter 6) and work on accepting others as they are. If you aren't used to being around people, the experience can be stressful and tense at first, but it'll become easier with time.

Relax About Meeting People

If you've isolated yourself or you're fearful of being with people, preparing to socialize is important for success. You don't have to begin developing connections by being in a group where you're expected to mingle and talk. Take small steps, such as sitting in the library or walking around a mall or other public area to just be around people. This can begin to lower your anxiety and help you prepare to interact at a later date.

Connecting with other people is difficult when you're anxious. Your brain is on guard and you're tense, which doesn't lead to being open and easygoing. The following exercise can help you relax about meeting people.

Riding Out Your Anxiety

Imagine yourself on an outing that would normally cause you moderate to high social anxiety, perhaps going to the grocery store or to a small party. Allow yourself to feel the anxiety you'd experience in this situation, without distracting or comforting yourself. Notice upsetting thoughts that increase your fear. Your anxiety level will rise when you start, but after perhaps a few minutes, it'll level off and start to fall. After a pre-set period of time or once you notice you're feeling much less anxious, do one of the progressive relaxation or breathing exercises in chapter 2 to further decrease your body tension. Do this a few different times on different days, until your anxiety is less intense.

Then go to the park, the library, or some other place that's not too threatening but makes you at least moderately anxious (but not severely anxious) about being around people. You may want to choose a busy time, when there are a lot of people. Again, let your anxiety rise, but stay with the feeling. Don't pretend you're somewhere else, think about other things, or do anything else to not feel the anxiety. Again, after a set period of time or after your anxiety has gone down significantly, do one of the progressive relaxation or breathing exercises from chapter 2 or use another method to further decrease your anxiety. Keep going back and repeating this until the situation makes you feel only slightly to moderately anxious. As time goes on, you'll find that you're less tense around people (Borkovec and Costello 1993; Myers and Davis 2007).

This practice can be quite challenging. Consulting a therapist who is knowledgeable about exposure therapy is likely to be helpful.

Practice Being Friendly

Once being in the presence of others is less overwhelming, the next step is to work on friendliness. Your body language is just as important as what you say, so pay attention to your posture and manner. If you express that you're happy to meet someone but your face looks terrified, that person isn't going to believe your words.

Watch yourself in a mirror. First, think scary thoughts about being with people and observe your face. Then think about someone you really like or a place you like to be. Practice in front of the mirror until you have a relaxed body posture and a welcoming smile. The more approachable you seem, the more positively others will respond to you.

Go to a familiar, open public place. Keep your face up, and smile as you walk. Remember the posture you practiced at home. Nod to adults or greet them with something simple, such as "Nice day, isn't it?"

When you can smile and greet with minimal discomfort, try doing so in a less familiar place or a more intimate setting—a small store, for example. Then try it everywhere you go.

Know that any time you feel disconnected, whether with your life partner or in a crowd of people, simply reaching out with a greeting or sharing a smile can help.

Making Connections with People

There are many ways to connect with people, including developing reciprocity, learning small talk, and rekindling old relationships. Before you can do any of those things, however, you may need to overcome your isolation.

In-Person Volunteer Work

If you've been isolated, in-person volunteer work is a great way to get out of your shell. You might volunteer with babies and young children or with people in need. Your local hospital may have a program in which volunteers rock babies whose mothers cannot tend to them. Shelters or group homes for youngsters always need volunteers. While young children can be painfully honest (for instance, they may ask why your ears stick out), they're also accepting. Adults in need, such as nursing home residents or the homeless, can also benefit from your contribution of time. Your church or place of worship, if you have one, likely has a way for you to be involved with people in need.

When you help others, it's easier to make a connection with them. The risk of being rejected or hurt in relationships with people you're helping and with your fellow volunteers is lower than with people you meet randomly. And while it may not be to the level of your ultimate goal, it's a step toward having more friends. It may also be an opportunity to practice receiving—for example, receiving thanks, compliments, and other shows of appreciation—as well as giving, which leads to reciprocity.

Developing Basic Reciprocity

Particularly in the beginning, relationships are typically built through reciprocity: taking and giving in roughly equal amounts (Haidt 2006). Being primarily either a "taker" or a "giver" can leave you with an empty, lonely feeling and keep you from developing healthy relationships.

IF YOU'RE A "TAKER"

If you're primarily a "taker," your interactions typically focus too much on what *you* are feeling and experiencing. While friends naturally share experiences, listen to, and reassure one another, you may need that support more often than most people. You may rely on your loved ones to help you feel better or help you manage your emotions more frequently than is comfortable for them. In fact, you may not know how to stop needing so much from others.

When you need too much in relationships, it's usually because you have difficulty managing your emotions and feel desperate to decrease your pain. Turning to others for help may be the only way you've learned to feel better, gain control, and solve problems. If so, then consider talking with a therapist who can help you learn new ways of coping. You can also practice the skills discussed in previous chapters, particularly chapters 2 and 5.

IF YOU'RE A "GIVER"

If you're a "giver," as many emotionally sensitive people are, you're uncomfortable with accepting help or gifts, and you deplete yourself at the cost of making others happy. You find your interactions with others emotionally fatiguing because you're constantly focused on how to help them, entertain them, or solve problems for them. You have a hard time saying no to your family and friends, and as a result they can seem like burdens rather than sources of support. You worry about people's feelings and act as if your relationships depend on your keeping others happy. At the same time, you may resent that others don't seem to consider your needs and feelings.

When you give too much, you may feel as lonely and empty as if you had no connections. To create some balance, set aside time for activities that are about you and what you want to do. You may find you don't know what to do. In that case, you may want to take a yoga class, keep a manicure appointment, take a writing or art class, or join a book club to see what gives you joy. Also, commit to accepting help and input from others. Let someone help you write a report for work, bake cookies for a party, or take care of a sick relative.

Learning Small Talk

For emotionally sensitive people, small talk can seem meaningless. You may often wonder, why bother chatting about the weather or local news stories? Yet if you dive right into highly personal matters as soon as you meet a new friend for coffee, your new friend may squirm or suddenly remember he has somewhere else to be. It's the norm to open a conversation with small talk, as a way to make people feel more comfortable discussing deeper, more intimate issues. Small talk is also a way of acknowledging other people, letting them know they matter, and exploring whether you have common interests. So if you're willing to take a deep breath and trudge through some short-term discomfort, small talk can help you see who holds the potential for deeper, more meaningful interactions. Here are a few ideas to help you get better at chitchat.

LEARN THE RHYTHM OF CONVERSATION

Both the pace and style of conversation are important when connecting with people. Talking too much or too little, as well as revealing too much or not enough personal information, can make the road to friendship more difficult.

Some people can chat for hours without stopping. Others are often at a loss for words and tend to answer using short phrases. Effective conversation, even small talk, is reciprocal. Try to give information or pose a question in about three to five sentences and then pause for the other person to contribute.

If you're a person of few words, listen carefully to what the other person is saying. Ask questions or make a comment, even if the topic is outside your interests. Show curiosity about what he or she likes and dislikes, not just what you have in common. If the conversation is about opinions, you can disagree and still acknowledge and show appreciation for the other person's stance. Remember to practice being nonjudgmental about his or her ideas and preferences.

Many friendships are based on shared activities. When meeting people, practice bringing up topics that interest you. Don't wait until you're comfortable to talk about your interests and hobbies—comfort comes with practice. Allude to movies, cooking, sports, your pets, books, volunteering, or whatever you like to do. Keep it light and upbeat.

At the same time, know that divulging too much personal information too soon interrupts the rhythm of building a conversation and a relationship. Oversharing can make the other person uncomfortable. For example, it's not ideal to tell someone you just met that you're seething because you got a bad job review earlier that day. However, if you're experiencing intense emotions, it may feel "phony" or wrong to talk about something else. Use skills you learned in chapters 2, 4, 5, and 7 to manage your emotions so that you can stay in the natural flow of a new relationship.

Remember that you want to create reciprocal, long-term relationships. Focus on that goal rather than the annoyances or urges of the moment.

Reconnecting with People: Reconsidering Past Relationships

If you're emotionally sensitive, it can be difficult to remember that most often the conflicts you have with others aren't worth giving up the relationship. If you've lost valued relationships for reasons that, in hindsight, didn't justify never talking to a person again, then an effort to reconnect may be worthwhile.

You may feel nervous and embarrassed to call a friend you haven't contacted for a while. Picking up the phone will be hard. Perhaps you imagine that your friend thinks negatively of you or must have been hurt by your neglect. You're taking a chance of being rejected, that the other person won't want to reconnect. In addition, your sense of justice may get in your way. You may wonder why *you* should be the one to make the effort, particularly if you view the other person as being responsible for the disconnect. Being more specific about what you'll do to check out the possibility of reconnecting may help you follow through.

Calling "just to talk" may be the least effective strategy, as it may not even lead to what you really want to talk about and can be awkward if neither of you knows the other's intention or knows what to say. Instead, decide on a way of expressing your feelings and your interest in reconnecting that will invite a response. Send a card saying you miss him or her and explaining how you've addressed your part of the issues that damaged the relationship; include an apology with a small gift; or call to wish him or her a happy holiday or birthday.

If the other person responds, then you'll likely discuss at least briefly the reason for the rift between you. Though a strong sense of justice may tempt you to point out the other person's mistakes, only address what you believe to be your own mistakes. It's possible the other person won't apologize for his or her part of the problem. That doesn't have to mean the relationship is unsalvageable. In any long-term relationship, you need to be willing to simply move past some mistakes and difficulties.

Maintaining Connections with People

Ongoing relationships require a conscious investment of time, communication, energy, and patience. Learning to say no and managing rejection sensitivity are key to your long-term success in this arena.

Saying No

You may have difficulty saying no, or you may say it too often. You may say it so timidly that others don't listen, or you may say it so harshly that you seem angry. You may give lots of reasons for refusing a request or invitation, or you may over-apologize for not being able to say yes, either of which creates awkwardness and tension (Linehan 1993).

If you aren't sure whether you want to say yes or no, make a pros and cons list. Weighing each specific pro and con according to how important each is to you will help you gain clarity. Most of the time, though, you'll already know the answer you want to give. The issue is that your emotions make it difficult. If this is the case, the ideas discussed in chapter 7 might be helpful.

The difficulty you have with saying no may often be about the associations you have with the word. You may see "no" as a rejection, evidence of a lack of caring, or a power play. You may fear that if you say no to someone, it might lead that person to abandon you.

Sometimes not saying no may be about wanting to maintain an image, such as being superhuman, able to meet all needs and requests. Or you may want to be perceived as being a kind and giving person at almost any cost. Recognizing the myths you have about saying no will help you improve your refusal skills.

SAY A CLEAR NO

When you say no, say it clearly, with resolve behind your words. Make eye contact, and keep your voice firm yet easygoing. Being indirect will make for a weak no, so choose your words carefully. For example, "I don't want to intrude" can elicit a response such as "It's no problem." A clear no is hard to counter. Most likely, you prefer people who are softly direct with you, and that's usually the most effective way to speak with others.

Keep it simple. Long explanations can make the interaction awkward. "No, that doesn't work for me" or "No, I can't do that" is simple, direct, and effective, especially when said in a caring manner.

Any time you're struggling with how to respond to a request, ask for time to think. That will allow you to calm your emotions and consider your response more carefully. If you're experiencing intense emotions, you're likely to give whatever answer will decrease your discomfort, and you may regret such an answer later.

NO IS A CHOICE

Keep in mind your refusal is not a gauge of how much you care about someone. You're simply stating you prefer not to do something.

Remember that saying no when you want to do so is a way of respecting yourself, your choices, and your goals. Self-respect will help you live a contented life. Time spent doing activities you don't want to do is time you'll never get back. In addition, it may foster resentment and other difficult emotions.

LET OTHERS KNOW TO EXPECT A DIFFERENCE

When you first begin to say no more frequently, family members and friends may react negatively. Because they're used to you agreeing, they may say that you "used to be so nice" and they don't understand what has happened to you. That can be discouraging. If this happens, keep in mind that they're probably reacting more to the change in your style of communicating than to your saying no. You can help soften such misunderstandings if you inform your friends and family members in advance you're working on saying no and ask for their support.

Accepting No

You'll have many opportunities to practice accepting no from other people. Some weeks it may seem as if "no" is all you hear. For example, you're turned down for a job, your friend says no to dinner, the owner of the house you want to buy refuses your offer, and your spouse won't agree to your poker group playing at your home.

Some refusals will be more difficult to hear than others. Any time you feel vulnerable when asking someone for something, hearing no is likely to result in hurt, disappointment, shame, embarrassment, or anger. You may feel strong emotions even when what you were asking for wasn't particularly important to you.

One of the most difficult situations is accepting no from someone you love. You may believe that if someone loves you, then that person should say yes to whatever you want, as long as your request is within reason. Sometimes you may fear that if your loved one says no to a simple request, then he or she might say no to something that really matters or he or she doesn't really love you. Hurt and fearful, you may tell yourself *That's the last time I ask for anything* and put up a wall of anger.

If the no is from a boss or a business partner, you may think of yourself as inadequate or perhaps a failure. Or you may be angry at the person who said no, judging him or her as selfish or as having some other negative characteristic.

Sometimes hearing no hurts because it seems unfair. Maybe you never or rarely ask for anything from your loved ones, and so it feels as though when you do they should say yes. In that case, realize that their no is only a response to your question or request for help, not a judgment of whether it's fair for you to ask.

Thinking in extremes can trap you into believing that getting whatever you're asking for is the only possible way you could be happy. Sometimes you may be so desperate that you attempt to control people and get them to concede to your requests. You may threaten certain actions or withdraw in anger. You might believe that if people just understood what a request means to you, they'd grant it, or if they just loved you enough, they'd do what you're asking.

By reacting in a negative way to someone saying no, you limit that person's freedom to choose. People who say no are just answering a question about whether they'll do something. For example, your wife didn't hear, "Do you love me?" She heard, "Will you go with me to visit my mother?" They don't see your request as a measure of how they feel about you. When you react as if their saying no is a rejection of you, others will learn to be careful about what they say to you. They may avoid answering you directly, make excuses, and not be honest. When this happens, part of the intimacy in the relationship is lost.

Sometimes you may be upset about hearing no because you're asking the other person to do something that seems critical to your well-being. Maybe, though, you're asking him or her to do something you aren't willing to do yourself. If that's the case, then learning or committing to do it for yourself will be a gift to you and the other person. For example, maybe you frequently ask a family member to help you cancel the lunch plans you make with friends. You may be upset if your family member says no, yet canceling your lunch plans may be a task you need to do yourself.

Do You Have Rejection Sensitivity?

If you're emotionally sensitive, you may be especially vulnerable to rejection. You may have difficulty managing your emotional reactions not only when you're actually rejected, but also when you sense rejection, and even when you merely anticipate rejection. You may frequently interpret others' behavior to mean you aren't valued or wanted, whether or not that was their intention. If someone expresses that he or she doesn't share your likes and dislikes, you may interpret it to mean that person doesn't want to be friends with you. If someone declines your invitation to meet for coffee or is late, you may see that as not valuing your friendship. Your relationships are like roller-coaster rides, because whenever you experience a lack of acceptance, you react with hurt and anger and pull away, only to return when you see yourself as accepted again. The cycle is a painful one, and it may confuse people or cause them to see you as too high-maintenance. However, there are some steps you can take to ease the suffering.

First, be aware of how rejection sensitivity affects you. If you believe you're rejection sensitive, then keep that possibility in mind when you're struggling with a relationship. Second, contribute to conversations and other social activities, because if you hold back or exclude yourself, you'll increase your feelings of not belonging and could see that as rejection by others. Finally, any time you think you've been rejected, push yourself to think it through more carefully:

1. Be mindful of your reactions. Take a pause and let your emotions settle before responding to a person you believe has rejected you.

2. Consider alternate explanations to rejection of you. What other reasons could there be for the other person's behavior? Think of at least three. Consider the facts of the other person's life. A mother with three young children may not have time to chat on the phone, however much she may want to talk with you.

3. If you can, calmly ask the person about his or her intention.

Being Right vs. Doing What Works

In relationships, you often have a choice between proving you're right about the facts or choices and doing what works to strengthen your connection (Linehan 1993). It's easy to become caught up in a win/lose frame of mind, especially if you have a strong sense of justice. Maybe you become so focused on proving your point that you forget that winning an argument isn't worth hurting the feelings of those you love. Or maybe you never assert yourself for fear of hurting the other person's feelings and often think that no one listens to you. Either extreme isn't helpful for relationships.

Perhaps you think that if you can prove you were right, then the other person shouldn't be upset about losing the argument. If so, think back to the times you've had disagreements and proven yourself right at the cost of someone else's feelings. Your being right doesn't help the other person feel better. Though you can say you didn't do anything wrong, you still took a risk with someone you cared about. Maybe you even lost the relationship. Jessica's story illustrates how a preoccupation with being right can ruin a relationship.

> Jessica was shocked when her husband asked for a divorce—she had no idea how unhappy he was. Only later did she understand that there had been no single big event that changed their relationship, but rather a series of small episodes.

> Jessica's husband complained that she always had to be right. He explained that when they were out with friends, she frequently corrected the small mistakes he made in telling stories about trips they had taken. She thought she was helping him tell the stories accurately. Her intention wasn't to push him away. But it didn't matter, because the experience of being repeatedly corrected was belittling to him. As a result, he enjoyed her company less. Her habit of quibbling over the veracity of small details damaged her marriage.

Focusing on being right is not the best approach to mutually beneficial relationships. Being effective is about knowing what works and what moves you closer to your goals. If Jessica wanted to strengthen her relationship with her husband, then her behavior wasn't effective.

To be effective in relationships, you have to consider the views of others. Let's say you get to choose how to divide an inheritance among you and your siblings. If your goal is to preserve your relationships with your brothers and sisters, you must take their views on what's fair into account. Simply dividing the inheritance based on what you think is fair won't work if your brothers and sisters don't agree.

In deciding whether it's better to be right or to be effective, you also have to understand the reality of the situation. Believing that it isn't right that the money you earn from babysitting counts as taxable income makes no difference to the IRS. Being adamant that it isn't right for your son to be fined for punching someone who was taunting him won't help you resolve the situation. If you're stuck on what's fair and what's not fair, you may make decisions that aren't in your best interest. For example, if you're applying to a college, and you think it's unfair for the college to give assignments for freshmen to complete prior to admission, you may decide not to do the work. You may think you're right, but the result is you're denied entrance. Unless you wanted to avoid attending the college, that choice was not an effective one.

Keep in mind that many things you may feel strongly about, such as your religious beliefs and political views, are opinions that can vary among individuals. Emotionally sensitive people can be quite passionate and forget that the manner in which they state what they believe has the potential to harm their relationships. If you want to build strong relationships, you'll need to be accepting of beliefs and views you don't agree with. When you express to someone an opinion that differs with his or hers, try to do so without criticizing. Look for the truth in the other person's point of view, show respect for the way he or she perceives the situation, and be gentle in the ways you communicate your ideas.

How Worry Can Damage Relationships

Emotionally sensitive people can be world-class worriers. You may see worry as being part of love and caring. Yet, worry can damage your relationships.

Worrying Can Drain Happiness

When your loved ones tell you good news, your worries may dampen their excitement. Often, good news means changes and risks, and that can be scary.

Imagine that your daughter tells you that she's been accepted to the college of her dreams. You secretly hoped she wouldn't be admitted because the college is so far away and there's a good local school she could attend. You bite your lip and say in a strained voice: "That's great. Congratulations." It's not long, though, before you furrow your brow and say, "If you go there, you won't be able to come home very often." You don't mean to decrease her excitement. You just want her to think of all the problems she'll encounter being so far away. You're also thinking about how much you don't want her to leave home. She may respond with "Mom, can't you just be happy for me? Just this once?"

Worry Communicates Lack of Confidence in Others

Though you may not mean it to, expressing worry about someone (intentionally or unintentionally—for example, through nonverbal behaviors) can communicate a lack of confidence in his or her choices and abilities. Your worry may convey that you don't think your friend or family member is capable of doing what he or she wants to do or is otherwise making a poor decision.

Worrying to Avoid Happiness

Sometimes people who worry are afraid of being happy. You may believe that if you allow yourself to be happy, something will happen to take the feeling away, and losing that feeling will hurt more than not having it in the first place. So when an event occurs that brings happiness, you may automatically look for ways it might not be a pleasant experience. Sometimes you do this for other people too, perhaps not even aware of what you're doing. For example, when something good happens for a friend, you may remind him of the many ways something could go wrong.

Although a realistic view considers both the advantages and challenges of situations, not celebrating or enjoying the positive events in your life (and others') will limit your overall happiness. Joining with others to celebrate joyful events is part of having a sense of belonging.

Worry Affects the Way Others Treat You

When you express frequent worries, others may see you as someone who can't handle life. Your friends and family members may say "Don't tell her—she'll just worry about it." They may discount your input on situations because they see you as a worrier. If others don't listen to you, or they keep secrets, that can lead you to feel left out, which may weaken or harm your relationships.

When others don't let you know what's happening, you may begin to worry about what they aren't telling you. That reaction will keep the cycle going, as others will continue to see you as unable to handle difficult facts or situations.

Ideas for Change

You may be confused by how others react to your worrying about them. If others don't seem to appreciate how much you care, or if you've noticed that your worry is pushing people away, then you may want to try to decrease your worry by using some of the following suggestions.

Find ways to be more aware of worry statements you make. For example, ask others to point out your worry behavior to you. Or count the number of worry statements you make throughout a day. Worrying may be such a habit that you don't notice how often you express your worry.

When you notice yourself expressing worry, be aware if there's a certain way that you stand, a particular look on your face, or a specific tone of voice. Knowing how you tend to express worry will help you be more aware of when you're doing it. If you notice that you're tense when you express worry, then practice changing your facial expression to a more relaxed one. Keep an even tone of voice, and remember to breathe deeply to relax your body.

Maybe you could identify the words and statements you typically use when expressing worry, then try to avoid them. Replace those expressions with supportive and congratulatory ones, such as "I'm so happy for you." You'll probably still have worries, but you won't always feel the need to express them.

If you do need to voice a concern, timing is important. If someone receives good news or has just made an important decision, first you should express happiness or excitement for that person. If the situation isn't urgent, let some time pass before you bring up the problems you see. Evaluate the reason for your worry: Do you have a logical reason to be concerned, or is your discomfort based only on emotions? If your reservations about the other person's decision aren't based on facts, then use the skills discussed in chapter 2 to manage your feelings.

Moving into Deeper Connections

Developing close relationships requires that you be open and vulnerable, be accepting of others, and communicate mindfully. When you form deeper connections with people, the risk of emotional pain is higher, but the benefits are also greater. Having thousands of "friends" on social networking websites isn't the same as having someone to watch a movie with you. A friend you meet periodically for coffee is different from someone who cares about your heartaches and successes and on whom you can depend when you're sick or need help.

Trust

If you're emotionally sensitive, maybe you've learned to sense and become what others want you to be. Taking on roles is exhausting. When you're trying to be whom others want you to be, you can't form true connections. So part of developing relationships is figuring out your identity (see chapter 8) and letting others see the real you.

Connecting requires being open to sharing who you are—your thoughts, opinions, likes, dislikes, values, strengths, and weaknesses—in a healthy way. That means gradually letting yourself be more vulnerable as you and another person develop trust in each other. Protect yourself by not sharing too much until the other person shows trustworthiness through valuing the relationship, being respectful of what's important to you, and generally keeping his or her promises to you. Keep in mind that your relationship won't move forward if you remain overprotected.

To keep the relationship developing at a good pace, stay mindful of how open the other person is being. Gradually share more about yourself while at the same time learning about the other person. Any time you're too open too soon, you'll likely have a queasy feeling. You may even say to yourself *I shouldn't be saying this much so soon*. That's probably your intuition working, letting you know you're making yourself more vulnerable than the relationship is ready for.

You'll notice the same internal nudge when you're not being open enough. You'll likely notice an imbalance in the amount of sharing going on. Perhaps the other person will comment about not knowing much about you. When this is the case, think about what the other person has shared with you. Consider sharing the same type of information about yourself.

Accept Others' Humanness

Being in relationships means accepting you'll be hurt at times. Even in the best of relationships, people will make decisions you don't appreciate and say things that upset you. In most cases, they don't intend to cause you distress. If you can assume with wisdom that your friends don't intend to hurt you, then you'll find it easier to work these situations out or let them pass so that the relationship endures.

Focus on enjoying your interaction rather than letting the other person's choices disrupt the relationship. For example, perhaps you meet a friend for dinner and feel annoyed because you don't like the restaurant she chose. You become so focused on your annoyances—the unappealing food, the noise, and so on—that you cannot enjoy the evening. You blame your friend. But what if when you noticed your irritation, you had asked yourself what was more important—maintaining and strengthening your relationship with your friend, or complaining about her choice of restaurant? Then you could have used the strategies you learned in previous chapters to manage your irritation.

Just as important as being able to let small annoyances go is the way you express your concerns about more important issues. Remember to calm your emotions before communicating, and put the relationship first. Watch your choice of words (avoid extremes, for example, such as "always" and "never"), and try to maintain a light and easy style that conveys care for the other person. This will give you the best chance of being heard and understood and will contribute to a constructive atmosphere.

Putting It All Together

A sense of belonging is a human need, just like the need for food and shelter. Feeling as if you belong, and trusting that you can maintain intimate relationships, will help you see value in life and cope with intensely painful emotions.

If you're emotionally sensitive, you probably tend to react to others' mistakes, perceived shortcomings, and unintended slights quickly and intensely. If you want to maintain connections with people, you'll need to come to terms with the fact that relationships can be messy. After all, no one is perfect. Changing how you interact with others will require active effort, time, practice, and consistent acceptance. Using the ideas in this chapter can help you manage your emotions more effectively, discover a sense of belonging, and create deeper, more satisfying relationships.

References

Ariely, D. 2012. *The Honest Truth About Dishonesty: How We Lie to Everyone—Especially Ourselves*. New York: Harper.

Baumeister, R. F., E. Bratslavsky, M. Muraven, and D. M. Tice. 1998. "Ego Depletion: Is the Active Self a Limited Resource?" *Journal of Personality and Social Psychology* 74: 1252–65.

Borkovec, T. D., and E. Costello. 1993. "Efficacy of Applied Relaxation and Cognitive-Behavioral Therapy in the Treatment of Generalized Anxiety Disorder." *Journal of Consulting and Clinical Psychology* 61: 611–19.

Brach, T. 2004. *Radical Acceptance: Embracing Your Life with the Heart of a Buddha*. New York: Bantam Books.

Cacioppo, J., and W. Patrick. 2008. *Loneliness: Human Nature and the Need for Social Connection*. New York: W. W. Norton and Company.

Cartwright, R. 2010. *The Twenty-Four Hour Mind: The Role of Sleep and Dreaming in Our Emotional Lives*. New York: Oxford University Press.

Conley, C. 2012. *Emotional Equations: Simple Steps for Creating Happiness in Business + Life + Success*. New York: Free Press.

Dweck, C. 2006. *Mindset: The New Psychology of Success*. New York: Random House.

Frey, W. 1985. *Crying: The Mystery of Tears.* With M. Langseth. Minneapolis: Winston Press.

Haidt, J. 2006. *The Happiness Hypothesis: Finding Modern Truth in Ancient Wisdom.* New York: Basic Books.

Halliman, J. 2010. *Why We Make Mistakes: How We Look Without Seeing, Forget Things in Seconds, and Are All Pretty Sure We Are Way Above Average.* New York: Broadway Books.

Heath, C., and D. Heath. 2013. *Decisive: How to Make Better Choices in Life and Work.* New York: Crown Business.

Kabat-Zinn, J. 1994. *Wherever You Go, There You Are: Mindfulness Meditation for Everyday Life.* New York: Hyperion.

Kross, E., M. Berman, W. Mischel, E. Smith, and T. Wager. 2011. "Social Rejection Shares Somatosensory Representations with Physical Pain." *Proceedings of the National Academy of Science* 108: 6270–75.

Lieberman, M. D. 2006. "Social Cognitive Neuroscience: A Review of Core Processes." *Annual Review of Psychology* 58: 259–89 (Volume publication date January 2007). First published online as a Review in Advance on September 26, 2006. doi: 10.1146/annurev.psych.58.110405.085654.

Linehan, M. 1993. *Cognitive Behavioral Treatment of Borderline Personality Disorder.* New York: Guilford Press.

McGonigal, K. 2012. *The Willpower Instinct: How Self-Control Works, Why It Matters, and What You Can Do to Get More of It.* New York: Avery.

McRaney, D. 2011. *You Are Not So Smart: Why You Have Too Many Friends on Facebook, Why Your Memory Is Mostly Fiction, and 46 Other Ways You're Deluding Yourself.* New York: Penguin Group.

Myers, K. M., and M. Davis. 2007. "Mechanisms of Fear Extinction." *Molecular Psychiatry* 12: 120–50. doi:10.1038/sj.mp.4001939. PMID 17160066.

Nezu, A., C. Nezu, and T. D'Zurilla. 2007. *Solving Life's Problems: A 5-Step Guide to Enhanced Well-Being.* New York: Springer.

Page, J., and P. Rhodes. 2012. *Freedom from Loneliness: 52 Ways to Stop Feeling Lonely*. Seattle: Amazon Digital Services.

Pink, D. 2005. *A Whole New Mind: Why Right-Brainers Will Rule the Future*. New York: Riverhead Books.

Rabinovitz, J. 2012, Spring. "Brain Power: Psychiatry Turns to Neuroscience." *Stanford Medicine Special Report*.

Randall, D. K. 2012. *Dreamland: Adventures in the Strange Science of Sleep*. New York: Norton.

Ratey, J. 2008. *Spark: The Revolutionary New Science of Exercise and the Brain*. With E. Hagerman. New York: Little, Brown and Company.

Rosenthal, R., and L. Jacobson. 1963. "Teachers' Expectancies: Determinants of Pupils' IQ Gains." *Psychological Reports* 19: 115–18.

Ross, L. 1977. "The Intuitive Psychologist and His Shortcomings: Distortions in the Attribution Process." In *Advances in Experimental Social Psychology*, vol. 10, edited by L. Berkowitz. New York: Academic Press.

Siegel, R. 2010. *The Mindfulness Solution: Everyday Practices for Everyday Problems*. New York: Guilford Press.

Steele, C. M. 2010. *Whistling Vivaldi and Other Clues to How Stereotypes Affect Us*. New York: Norton.

Wilson, K. G., and T. DuFrene. 2010. *Things Might Go Terribly, Horribly Wrong: A Guide to Life Liberated from Anxiety*. Oakland, CA: New Harbinger Publications.

Wilson, T. 2011. *Redirect: The Surprising New Science of Psychological Change*. New York: Little, Brown and Company.

Karyn D. Hall, PhD, is the director of the Dialectical Behavior Therapy Center in Houston and a DBT Trainer/Consultant with Treatment Implementation Collaborative. She is the coauthor of *The Power of Validation* and is on the Board of Directors for National Education Alliance Borderline Personality Disorder (NEA.BPD).